REVIEWS

"This debut memoir presents a modern-day, rags-to-riches story that articulates the concepts employed by the author to overcome his personal demons.

Bowers, "a boy born into blue-collar beginnings," progressed "from a secondhand start" and a "lackluster adulthood" to being a millionaire by the age of 28. His early years were fraught with anxiety over his parents' constant fights and poverty: "Our lives consisted of hand-me-downs, handouts, and empty pockets; we lived a paycheck-to-paycheck lifestyle." In elementary school, as he saw how his friends' families lived (he was raised in upscale communities), he began building "walls" to protect himself "from ridicule and embarrassment." Adding to the family's tribulations was his older brother, Billy, who was constantly in jail for a variety of crimes. High school provided the author with a period of stability: "I was one of the popular kids, liked by almost everyone." He had a girlfriend, played on the school's baseball team, and worked as a bus boy at night for some much-needed money. But with his friends off to college and no clear goals, Bowers crashed after high school. While working as a janitor in a motel, he met Yuka and fell in love. A curveball—an unexpected baby—became the motivation the 22-year-old needed to set himself on the road to success. While the author recalls that "nothing was ever given to me for free" and he remains critical of his mother and father ("My parents never knew how to budget money"), he seems to overlook the value of his childhood milieu, which raised his aspirations. Still, the captivating book's simple, straightforward prose effectively communicates the turmoil of young Bowers' life, the valuable steps he took to shed his glass-half-empty mindset, and the worthy lessons he learned along the way. Initially crafting this memoir to "vent" and "fan the flames of frustration" he felt toward his parents, the author skillfully expanded his mission: "Now I know I am writing it to release everything I've pent up within me, and to hopefully help others in the process."

An intriguing account that shows readers how to use life's difficulties to turn a negative self-image into a positive, goal-oriented one."

- Kirkus Reviews

JUN – – 2019

"This book is a touching story that shows how one overcame his struggles. We all can relate to Ace in one way or another and while reading this book you'll find yourself analyzing your own experiences and habits that might need changing."

"I must admit I was originally curious to read this book to see how a Janitor got to Silicon Valley millionaire in five years...Surprisingly, this is not that kinda book, and in a good way. It takes you through a journey about the American family and the trials that they all went through and experienced. It was a very personal and deep book, and it helps to give you a better perspective on the struggles people go through and how you can never judge a book by its cover. I highly recommend this book and once I started I couldn't put it down."

"*The Mindset*...This is a wonderful book and I highly recommend it. Reading this book really inspires me to work hard and it shows how to keep the right mindset to succeed even when you are at your lowest times. I went on an emotional roller coaster reading this book. Every chapter contains a great message. No matter what you are facing in life, this book teaches you how to not lose hope. It is very powerful."

"This is the story of a boy lost, who found himself through love and family, and a belief in God, that became a very successful Man. It's told honestly and fervently with a very happy ending. A refreshing read in a world where so many boys in his shoes never find the right path."

"I enjoyed reading this book. The author depicts many vulnerable childhood memories. His childhood poverty gave him the drive to overcome and want a better life for himself. The book was very interesting and I read it from cover to cover within a couple of hours. This book would be a good resource for underprivileged students to read, to encourage them to rise above their environmental circumstances, and give them initiative and hope for a better life."

"Wow! This book resonates with my life so much. From personal issues at home to personal struggles. I came up from nothing myself and I own 2 restaurants now. I love this book. Quick read but not so quick to digest. I recommend this book to anyone who struggles to get by, for hope and encouragement. Classic story from rags to riches with all of life's struggles. Thank you for this read!"

"*The Mindset* is a book written for, and notably by, The Everyman. Ace Bowers shares his all-too-familiar back story of a young man from a working class background, teetering on the edge of a financial and ultimately emotional abyss. He hides nothing from us, laying bare his internal monologue: the non-stop anxiety he felt as a child in a dysfunctional home, his constant feeling of worthlessness as a 21 year-old down-and-outer and his ensuing battle with depression. Wonderfully, Ace lifts himself and his family out of the abyss, chronicling the journey. But rather than focusing on the material trappings of success, he details his internal transformation-- this is where so many struggle and fail, and so many can learn from his example. Ultimately, *The Mindset* is a story of redemption, not just for Ace, but for his parents and brother as well. The author never gives up on himself, nor on them."

"The Mindset is a heartfelt, autobiographical story of a blue-collar kid from a blue-collar family growing up through a different kind of adversity; trying to make it in Silicon Valley and growing up in a dysfunctional family. Ace opens up and shares some very personal stories from his life that helped shape him into a man he is today. The main theme that runs throughout the book is that of overcoming; Overcoming abuse, depression, anxiety, and so much more. This is a story that makes you want to say "if this guy can make it with the hand his life dealt him... what's my excuse?" This story is so much more than a story of rising from rags to riches. This is a story where all of us can find something we can relate to. Ace and his story are undeniable proof that it is possible to rise above our circumstances with the tools we all have at our disposal. A great read."

"*The Mindset* is a phenomenal book that brings you back to the basics of what is truly important in life. Bowers effectively makes his reader feel like a fly on the wall, privy to the shame and embarrassment he felt through his entire childhood, and how that shaped the young adult he had become.

Growing up in Silicon Valley is truly a double-sided sword. There are endless jobs and growth potential, yes... but there is also a false sense of accomplishment and success that children feel they must possess through their parents. Like every child, Bowers takes his parents' hardships and addictions as a personal failure that leads to his own self-demise and depression.

In the current times of social media, and the feeling of presenting a false sense of happiness to belong, Bowers reminds us that the power to become successful lies within each of us and our own sheer determination. More so than his success financially, is the success he finds with his personal relationships and family. Bowers makes you realize how important it is to know that the only barrier preventing someone from becoming what they want to be, is not trying.

The Mindset is an uplifting story of overcoming hardship to become a happy, successful & satisfied adult through letting go of the pain of your childhood, forgiving your family, and making an effort to be present and an active participant in your own life. I'd highly recommend!"

THE MINDSET

My Journey

from Janitor

to Silicon Valley Millionaire

in Five Years

ACE BOWERS

Genre: Nonfiction Memoir
Author: Ace Bowers
Publisher: Amazon KDP
ISBN Soft Cover: 978-1-7329481-0-5
ISBN Ebook: 978-1-7329481-2-9
ISBN Audio Book: 978-1-7329481-2-9
Price: Paperback $11.99 / Ebook $6.99 / Audio Book $8.99
Date of Publication: March 16, 2019

ACKNOWLEDGEMENTS

Yuka - You saved me from rock bottom.

Noah - You were my new beginning.

Ariel - You are my lion of God.

CONTENTS

CHAPTER 1:   Blue-Collar Beginnings   1

CHAPTER 2:   Rock Bottom and a Mop Bucket   21

CHAPTER 3:   The Noah Effect   31

CHAPTER 4:   Footsteps into Fatherhood   37

CHAPTER 5:   Millionaire Moves   45

CHAPTER 6:   My Rock (Kokoro no sasae)   57

CHAPTER 7:   Band of Brothers: 61
             A tale of two roads

CHAPTER 8:   Reckless Abandon: 73
             The prodigal son never returns

CHAPTER 9:   Talking it Out: 79
             Conversations with my family

CHAPTER 10: Overcoming and Self-Reflection: 89
             Release it and let go

Introduction

One of my mom's favorite songs has always been "Simple Man," by Lynyrd Skynyrd, because it encompassed her greatest aspirations for me. "All I want for you, my son, is to be satisfied." Try as I might, and in spite of her best hopes for me, it would take me many long years to find this happiness...

It always starts the same: flashbacks roll like movie clips, triggered by just about anything. A whiff of a cigarette. The sound of people yelling. My children's laughter... Instantly I'm transported to a time in my life when I felt helpless, worthless, and ashamed.

I think of the room where my sister and I would take refuge from the brutal storm created by my parents' fighting. I think of the empty bedroom where my brother should have been, but instead all I see is the painful memory of him handcuffed, over and over again.

I ducked and dodged the never-ending curiosity of teenage life, knowing how at any moment, I could be the next rumor floating around school if anyone knew how we lived. The feeling of a mop bucket in one hand and a cigarette in another, I would look at my reflection in cloudy water and wonder, *was this all my future held?*

This book focuses on my early life and journey into adulthood. In some ways it encompasses the American Dream, and in other ways, a nightmare far too real to escape. I will walk you through a five-year turning point in my life, starting as a janitor who couldn't afford the cigarettes he was smoking and earning $6.00 per hour with no end in sight, to finishing as a young man with the conscientious determination to get his life together. Fast forward some more, and I am now a man with a great job, a father married to the woman he loves, and a millionaire living in one of the most expensive cities in the country.

CHAPTER 1
Blue-Collar Beginnings

My name is Ace and I am going to tell you the complete story of my journey. I was a boy born into blue-collar beginnings. I progressed from a secondhand start, to a lackluster adulthood, and somehow ended up rubbing elbows with white-collar millionaires. In a few short years, I finally became a millionaire myself. No, I didn't attend an Ivy League school, I didn't invent anything, and I didn't inherit wealth. Nothing was ever given to me for free. Everything I have today I earned by working hard.

I may not have been born into money or have things come easy for me, but what I did possess was *motivation*. This motivation would fuel my determination to break my cycle of poverty, and to create a strong mindset within myself. I now refer to it as an *overcomer's mindset*. I didn't know it then, but this mindset would change my life. It would allow me to develop my own system of learning; through it, I experienced a mature mental growth that would serve me well in my years to come. An unrelenting motivation and steady mindset would carry me further than anything else in my life would. It was through this unwavering state of mind that I could become a millionaire at 28 years old.

Climbing from minimum wage to millions was not the product of some lucky stars, nor was it easy. Some people say you make your own luck and others think that believing in luck is foolish, but my journey came through trial and error, full of ups and downs. From this journey, I discovered something paramount: nothing is *ever* a waste of time if you learn something from it. Even today, I continue to grow and develop from my successes and my failures. That bumpy road taught me how to become motivated, and this motivation would make great things happen for me. A great deal of willpower, persistence, and fortitude was involved—and of course, a helping hand from the man upstairs.

My journey would require change—lots of it. I had to change my thinking, my attitude, my outlook and my habits. I had to transform myself, especially the way I saw myself, and the preconceived notion that I would live the same life my parents had.

I've learned that motivation is powerful and you should never ignore the fire it can spark within. But let's back up. When I initially sat down to write this book, I soon came to the realization that I had buried many of my childhood memories. I was carrying them around like baggage, the weight of which took its toll. They left me suffocated and would result in bad decisions, a lack of drive, and an overall poor outlook on life. I am only now allowing myself to feel those memories and experiences again. This book marks my first venture into being openly frank about my life.

Many of the things I am going to tell you in this book, I have spent my entire life trying to forget. I wanted to hide these secrets from the world and I certainly never thought I'd be in a place where I could share the shame I felt with the world. No one knows the things you are about to read...

For a while growing up, I didn't understand the actual chaos of my environment and I didn't know what to think. I had no clue about success, because failure and instability were all around me. Unfortunately, I had no plans on doing anything noteworthy any time in the near future. We will talk more about that later but for now, back to the start of things.

There I was, growing up in Mountain View, California, just an average kid in a blue-collar family trying to scrape by. I was the son of two high school sweethearts who had never gone to college. My dad is a blue-eyed, patriotic, family-first man who loves baseball and working with his hands. His philosophy has always been God, family, and America. Dad grew up as a clean-cut, all-American star athlete from a middle-class family. My mother on the other hand, is his polar opposite. She grew up on the wrong side of the tracks: a free-spirited, non-judgmental, stereotypical 60's hippie with olive skin and an aversion to shoes. She never wore shoes, and to this day still loves to be barefoot. She doesn't share the same core values or political ideologies as my dad. Mom was, and still is, very liberal.

I was the youngest of three kids. The oldest was my brother and in the middle was my sister, who also happened to be my biggest advocate growing up. She protected and shielded me from some of the regularly-occurring madness happening at our house. Our lives consisted of hand-me-downs, handouts, and empty pockets; we lived a paycheck-to-paycheck lifestyle. That said, I do not remember elementary school being so bad in spite of our situation. I was aware from a young age that I was the poorest kid in school, but I did not dwell on materialistic possessions. Society would commonly refer to people of our status as white trash, but at that point I didn't concern myself with hiding my home life.

At that age, I didn't need to worry about hiding my real life from others. I've always made friends easily, and it wasn't until going to my friends' houses and meeting their families, that I started noticing how my home life and family were very different from theirs. And so, bit by bit, I began building my walls and hiding my true life from the world. As early as elementary school, I relied on my walls as a defense mechanism in order to protect myself from ridicule and embarrassment.

What I learned as a kid forced me to mature quickly and to let go of my childhood sooner than I should have. I realized that we were poor, lower class and always struggling. This was drastically different from what I'd seen at my other friends' houses. I found that my brother would grow increasingly absent from my life. He was constantly in and out of jail, and his rebellious ways would become a cloud that followed my family forever. I witnessed my parents abuse alcohol and tobacco and came to the realization that they couldn't manage money: their lack of financial discipline was the main reason we were poor.

Speaking of managing money, I could always tell how far away from payday we were by what we ate for dinner. The month would start out with normal family meals, but these would gradually taper off. If we were less than a week away from payday, our dinners would consist of dishes like creamed egg on toast, or "shit on a shingle," as my dad liked to call it. The term was from his Navy days—he always looked for a way to incorporate military slang into our lives. Hot dogs were also a recurring menu item, except our family couldn't afford buns: since we couldn't afford buns, we usually ate them on white bread. A child shouldn't have to notice these kinds of things, but I should give my mom credit. She always made the best with what she had.

As I mentioned before, my parents fought. My sister and I had front row seats and the privilege to witness the main event: their attempts at working out their issues. A lot of the things I experienced in my childhood stuck with me and not in a good way—*especially* their fights. Those experiences molded my personality, shaped my view of the world, and derailed my path into adulthood.

As I remember it, our housing was pretty stable until around 1992, when, at the age of eight, we moved from the house I was born in. We ended up quickly moving a few more times thereafter. I think my parents had fallen into the "interest only" home loan trap. When the rates skyrocketed, they could no longer afford their mortgage payments. To make things worse, when I was around ten years old, my dad was laid off from his job as a machinist at Stanford University, where he had worked for over a decade. This marked the first time I witnessed my family fall on hard times.

We moved in with my grandmother on my mom's side—my *Nanny*. During that time, I remember walking to the mailbox every day after school with my mom, to see if my dad's unemployment check had arrived. We needed his check to buy groceries, school supplies, and to get our car running again. It was the start of a new school year for me, and I can recall the other kids sporting new clothes, lunchboxes, fancy backpacks, and plenty of school supplies. Meanwhile, I had an old, beat up hand-me-down backpack with a broken zipper from my brother.

Other students would ask me why I didn't have school supplies or any new clothes, and I remember telling them that my parents were just too busy to go to the store. Of course, I knew the real reason: we couldn't afford anything. We didn't even have a car to go to the store. During this one-to-two month period, I would pray at night that my dad's unemployment check would come. When I was at school, I would convince myself that today would be the day it'd be in the mailbox when I came home. Raising my hopes, walking to the mailbox, and not seeing his check let me down in ways I can't explain. The unending disappointments of my situation deeply affected my outlook in life, and engraved in me a glass half-empty viewpoint that lingered throughout my childhood and a few years into my adulthood.

After a few months, when the check finally did arrive, my mom and I rushed to the bank so she could cash it. But we didn't have enough money in our bank account, and the bank would not cash his check. They would only deposit it with a 48-hour hold, with no exceptions because my parents had overdrawn too many times. I could see my mom's desperation as she quietly asked for the manager, not wanting to cause a scene. As the manager approached the counter, I could feel all eyes on us and the other bank patrons staring. He had a very matter-of-fact attitude and abruptly said, "Sorry ma'am, it's our policy. Have a nice day." This proved too much for my mom, who immediately started crying and sank to her knees right there on the bank floor.

Now, looking back, I realize how much she was relying on that check to pay bills that were already past due, but all I could do as a ten-year old boy was watch the scene unfold in front of me. This event served as a glimpse into my life, a preview of things to come, and it would affect me in ways I wasn't prepared for. I'll never forget the sinking feeling of dread and embarrassment that I felt, as the other patrons stared at us like we were beneath them—like we were garbage. It was in this very moment, I learned that people treat you differently based on how much money you had or did not have. Even to this day, no matter how wealthy I am, I don't like to go inside banks. In my mind, people who work at banks will always be "those people" who made me feel all of that shame as a young boy.

Shortly before starting 7th grade, we moved to Cupertino because my parents had found a house to rent. My dad had made an agreement—a barter—with the landlord: instead of calling the landlord for any repairs, my dad would take care of everything himself. Here I was in a new town, a new school, and I didn't know anyone. To give you some perspective, Cupertino is one of the wealthiest cities in America and serves as Apple's headquarters. The average income in this suburb is well above six figures, and the average education level for the parents of my "soon-to-be friends" was a graduate degree. My dad, on the other hand, had a blue-collar machinist job and learned his trade in the Navy. My mom had been a housewife ever since my brother was born on the Navy base when she was just seventeen. Unfortunately, kids in junior high are savvy enough to notice if another student is poor or not.

No matter where I lived or went to school, I was the poorest kid. It was protocol to always have an excuse ready any time a friend asked a personal question, and my friends regularly tried to break down or peek behind the protective wall I had built around myself to hide my personal life. There were always questions about my parents, how much my dad earned, and why our car was a twenty-year-old piece of crap minivan. Their parents drove new, high-end cars like BMWs or Mercedes-Benz.

I remember constantly begging my mom to drop me off a few blocks away from school because I was too ashamed of our family car, and didn't want to explain it to my friends. One day, it was pouring rain and my mom insisted on dropping me off right in front of school. I was a nervous wreck. What if my friends saw me? What if the girl I had a crush on saw me? I felt so anxious but she insisted, so I slouched down in the seat as far as I could when she approached the front of the school. As she pulled over to let me out, the car made a funny noise. I looked at my mom with dread in my eyes because I knew exactly what had just happened: the car was dead. It wouldn't start. I couldn't believe this was happening right in front of my school. I jumped out and could only hope that no one had recognized our car or my mother waiting for my dad to pick her up as I sprinted to class. I had an excuse at the ready and remained suspended, with baited breath, just in case any questions arose.

There were a lot of things in my life that I was constantly trying to hide from everyone else. At this age, kids are supposed to be carefree and learn how to live a happy life. Meanwhile, *my* top priority was to protect myself from possible ridicule, and to prevent anyone from coming close enough to see my real life. I couldn't let anyone know we rented a house, or that my parents never went to college, or that my *own brother* was in jail. I didn't want anyone to see that our family was barely scraping by. I surely didn't want anyone to know about my parents' drinking, and I never wanted anyone to see or hear them fight.

Let me shed some light on the tumultuous environment I'm talking about: both of my parents abused alcohol. This created an atmosphere of dysfunction where they fought constantly. These were not arguments, they were full-blown fights, and they happened *every single night*. It wasn't so bad when I had my sister there with me, but once she left for college, I was alone to weather their fights.

I was the chubby kid who used humor to deflect, and a

smile to hide my real pain. Back then, no one would think to correlate childhood trauma with depression, but it's clear that I began battling depression at this age. The instability, turbulent environment, state of constant worry, and fear created an everlasting feeling of uncertainty that made me into an emotional mess. This damaging environment began to sow the seeds of resentment towards my parents. I think there came a point when they dealt with so much financially and emotionally, that they stopped attempting to shelter me from these things altogether.

I felt cheated, robbed, and betrayed. I believed I was inferior, like I was lacking something, and I was always ashamed. Was this my problem? Was I being too hard on my family? Looking back, I had a roof over my head and food to eat, but I lived in despair. Maybe if my parents hadn't fought so much and hadn't drunk so much, I wouldn't feel this way today. Yet whenever I dwell on positive recollections of my childhood, I quickly realize that all the memories that should've been positive were *always* overshadowed by negative ones.

When I was around nine years old, we took a road trip to Los Angeles for a family reunion, and my dad knew that one of my childhood dreams was to visit Disneyland and stay in the Disneyland Hotel. Hotel guests could see all the rides from their room window. They had special access to the park and didn't have to waste time parking and walking. Just like Ralphie's desire to have a Red Ryder BB gun in *A Christmas Story*, the Disneyland Hotel offered a first-class experience that, for once in my life as a kid, I wanted a taste of. Of course, my dad told me that we probably couldn't afford to stay at the Disneyland Hotel; we would stay at the Motel 6 instead. Really, I was just grateful that I would go to the Happiest Place on Earth.

We arrived in Los Angeles for what should have been a weekend full of fun and happy memories for our family. On our first night, everyone was in the lobby of the hotel my aunt Cindi had booked a room at. It was higher-end lodging and certainly better than our motel. My parents had been drinking at the hotel bar and were fighting (as usual). My mom started yelling and crying, right there in that fancy hotel lobby, and I knew things had escalated to a breaking point when hotel security arrived. My aunt rushed my sister and me, along with her own kids, up to her room. After that, it's difficult to remember what happened, because all I could see was my mom sitting on the floor, her shoes in her hands.

I caught a glimpse of her from inside the elevator as the doors slid shut, and I thought to myself, *this* is my life. I didn't see my parents again until the following morning when we drove back home. They had ended the trip early. Needless to say, there would be no Disneyland for me this time. Fighting, disappointment, and embarrassment seemed to be a recurring theme all throughout my childhood. Every single time I would get my hopes up for something—for just a *glimpse* of a normal life—my parents would let me down once again. At that time, Disneyland was absolutely not the happiest place on earth.

In addition to my aunt, Nanny helped us out a lot. I never told my parents this, but the way I found out about Santa Claus was because one night, I overheard my dad asking Nanny if he could borrow some money from her to buy Christmas presents for me and my sister. In fact, on several occasions, I overheard him call and ask her or my aunt for rent money. As an adult and a father, I can only imagine how hard that was for him to do, having to swallow his pride and call his mother-in-law or his little sister to ask for rent money.

My parents never knew how to budget money (so it comes as no surprise that I couldn't figure it out for some time either). They always lived paycheck to paycheck. I would go with my dad on payday to cash his check at the liquor store, but instead of saving money he would waste it on chewing tobacco, cigarettes, and beer. Every week, without fail, he purchased these items, and I thought it was normal. I thought these were staples in everyone's household.

One of the most difficult questions for me to deflect, especially in high school, was why I never invited anyone over to my house. In high school, I always had friends and would often go over to their homes, but I never wanted to invite anyone over to mine. Their families would have me over for dinner, take me with them to the movies, and invite me to experience the typical things teenagers did. I could never reciprocate that.

One day in high school, I knew my parents weren't going to be home so I convinced myself that today, I could invite my three closest friends over after school. I went home early from school to make sure the house was clean and nothing embarrassing was sitting out—there could be no overdue bills visible on the counter and no ashtrays full of cigarette butts on the table. I was convinced that everything would be okay. I was wrong.

After about an hour into us three playing video games in the living room, our power was shut off because my parents hadn't been able to afford the bill. I knew immediately what had happened because this was in no way a rare occurrence. I knew my friends (having come from a more pampered lifestyle) probably didn't know what was going on right away, but I was already coming up with excuses just in case anyone asked questions: we had just switched cable companies. The neighbors were remodeling and must have cut the power line. Anything to hide the truth.

Growing up, my life consisted of three elements: my brother moving in and out of jail; my parents constantly fighting; and myself, living in fear that my friends would find out the truth about my life. All of this left me depressed and anxiety-ridden. Like a carousel, it was a cycle that went around and around, over and over every day without end. I operated in a constant state of fear as to what would happen next.

When I was about ten years old, my parents' fighting grew much worse and would remain so the entire time I lived with them. Keep in mind that my parents were high school sweethearts, married before my dad was drafted into the Navy. My mom had been only seventeen when she gave birth to my brother. Considering that she didn't work, and that they lived off my dad's meager earnings, I can appreciate that times were difficult for them. Now skip ahead to the years when my brother began going to jail. He started with petty crimes like drug possession and stealing, but as he got older, he graduated to selling drugs, becoming involved in gangs, possessing weapons, and drunk driving. Whatever money my parents had went directly to helping him, but it was never enough. I know this added pressure to an already fraught situation. Tensions mounted and mounted for years, and when I was ten, it hit a boiling point. I wouldn't move out of my parents' house until I was twenty years old, so the next ten years would be hell.

The fights were a nightly occurrence, like clockwork. During the day, my dad was usually at work and my mom stayed home cooking and cleaning. My mom is a very soft and gentle woman, very much the typical loving housewife and mother. But there existed a dark side, an unrecognizable side to her that came out when she drank. She was angry, vengeful and a totally different woman and unfortunately, she drank every night. Maybe it was her way of dealing with the daily stress of being broke, or maybe she let her buried resentment spill out when she was in a loose state of mind, but as soon as the sun went down and she began to drink, her alter ego came out and it never held back. Now, when my dad drinks, he is more even-keeled. Alcohol doesn't turn him into an angry drunk; he is the same person with the same temperament as when he is sober. He remains calm, relaxed, and pretty easygoing. This is probably why he allowed my mom to get away with abusing him.

As a kid, I learned to watch for certain patterns and behaviors that my parents would display to identify the signs that a fight was about to begin. My mom was always the instigator: as soon as she started drinking, she became increasingly passive aggressive and would do things very loudly, like clanking the dishes or stomping her feet as she walked by, persisting in doing these little things to irritate my dad. She would burn vanilla-scented candles or incense in the house, because she knew my dad hated the smell (to this day, I cannot stand the smell of vanilla because it brings back those memories). She'd make snide comments to my dad and do her best to try and agitate him. If he took the bait, she would explode, but if he didn't, she would keep at it until he was pushed to the limits. It was like watching someone pick at a scab so hard, it bled. It was *cruel*, and unrelenting.

Mom always tried to hide her drinking from me and my sister. She'd drink from a tumbler, one of those coffee mugs with a closed lid, so we couldn't see its contents. But we knew, just like how we knew that the sunglasses she wore indoors were to hide her bloodshot eyes, or how she would smoke cigarettes in the house when she was intoxicated. When she was sober, she always smoked outside or in the garage.

Every night as I fell asleep, I would listen to my parents fighting through the air vent in my bedroom—to this day, at home or at work, if I hear muffled voices through an air vent, I am transported back to that terrible place. These fights were unbearably disturbing for me to observe throughout my childhood. I saw my mother slap my father, hit him and throw things at him; thankfully I never once saw him hit her back. He mostly just tried to restrain her. She would often lock herself in the bathroom with a knife and threaten to kill herself. I developed an unfortunate habit, courtesy of my mom's multiple threats to harm herself, where I learned to instinctively check the cutlery block for missing knives when I came home from school. One night, she tried to kill herself by overdosing on my sister's medication. My dad called 911 and the police came and took her away. They put her on suicide watch. I will always remember standing in the driveway, watching the police car drive away with her in the back seat. The kind of impact this had on me as a young boy was detrimental. I'm an adult now, and even as I relive the things I went through, it doesn't get easier.

I was always very careful not to allow any friends over to my house at night—and for good reason. I still remember the worst fight. One of my best friends in 6th grade was named Jordan. Jordan was the only child of wealthy parents. I was always at his house and slept over most Friday or Saturday nights. I loved the feeling at his house—it was so peaceful and happy. I had nothing to worry about in this carefree environment, unlike my own home. Eventually, he asked me why I never invited him to spend the night at my house. I knew the reason but I couldn't tell him why. I made up excuses instead: My sister gets up very early and she might wake us up. My sister always has friends over and they hog the TV. But I knew it hurt his feelings that I never had him sleep over at my house.

So, I finally decided I needed to have him spend the night, at least once. I settled on a Saturday in the summertime, and I watched my parents closely all day looking for warning signs. As the afternoon progressed and the sun went down, I felt like tonight may be one of those rare nights when all would be alright. Convinced the coast was clear for a smooth evening, I picked up the phone at around 5 p.m. and called Jordan to invite him for a sleepover. I hung up the phone and thought, "Well, there's no turning back now!"

It turns out that I had misread the signs all wrong that day: it was the calm before the storm. That night would wind up being the worst night of my childhood. About an hour after the call, Jordan's mother dropped him off in front of my house. I hung out with Jordan while simultaneously keeping one eye and ear on my parents and the general mood of the house. Night had fallen and I was a nervous wreck, anxiously waiting on pins and needles to see how the evening would unfold.

Let me set the scene for you. My brother had been out of jail for a few weeks and was living on our couch. He was in the family room, playing video games and drinking. My sister, a high school senior at the time, was also home and in her room. My dad had been unemployed for a few months after being laid off from his last job due to budget cuts, and was drinking heavily to cope. My mom was acting... well, like my mom. They were both in their bedroom drinking and watching TV. Jordan and I were in my bedroom being kids. Then, out of nowhere, a loud crash resounded through the house and I jumped out of my skin. I panicked and tried to rationalize the bang. It was anything other than fighting—it *had* to be. Soon after, muffled voices resonated through the air vent in my bedroom. I knew trouble was coming, *but what could I do?*

I began thinking of excuses to tell Jordan to make him go home right away. Maybe if I told him I wasn't feeling good, he would call his parents to pick him up. But I was too late; before I could even finish a thought, a door slammed. Soon after, the yelling began. My parents were in the hallway now. I told Jordan I'd be right back and ran out of my room into the hallway, closing the door behind me. I tried to say something to my parents—I tried to stop them—but they wouldn't even acknowledge me. My sister, luckily, knew what was happening, and ushered Jordan to her bedroom near the back of the house. She was attempting to shield him from front row seats to the fight about to begin.

The fight quickly escalated and things became worse to the point where Jordan heard everything: the swearing, the crying, the shattering dishes. A few moments later, without understanding what had happened, I heard my brother yelling. I ran out into the hallway and realized that someone had punched a hole in the bedroom door. My dad and brother were now in a full-blown fist fight in the hallway. The next few minutes were a blur, but somehow my parents ended up in my bedroom fighting with each other. I remember crying hysterically, begging them to stop. I had a small Red Rider Daisy BB gun in my room, and in one final, desperate plea, I held it to my head and screamed that I was going to pull the trigger if they didn't stop. It didn't work. They didn't even notice me. Eventually, they left my room and kept fighting in the hallway. I sank to the floor in tears and just lay there in horror, knowing that Jordan could hear everything. I finally fell asleep right where I'd fallen.

The next morning, I was too afraid to leave my bedroom: what would I say to Jordan? I couldn't even look him in the eye. I cautiously stepped out my room and surveyed the house. There was a hole in my parents' bedroom door, the refrigerator drawers were lying broken on the floor, the stand up clock in the living room had been shattered to pieces... and Jordan sat at the kitchen table eating pancakes. *Pancakes.* My mom had made us pancakes, as if nothing had happened the night before. As if no one had punched a hole in the door, as if no one had shattered the clock. We never spoke of that night again—not me, not my parents, not my sister, not even Jordan. No one ever uttered a word about it. And I've never told anyone until now. As you probably guessed, that was the last time I ever had anyone sleep over at my house.

I am incredibly thankful to have had my sister during this period. With her, I wasn't alone during the times our parents were fighting, which seemed never-ending. It wasn't as bad with my sister there. She always protected me and reassured me that everything would be fine. I would seek refuge in her room during the altercations, and she would comfort me and tell me not to listen to them. She always reminded me that it *wasn't our fault.* Unfortunately, the fighting was worse after she left. We are five years apart in age, and she eventually went to college when she was eighteen. That left me home alone with my parents at thirteen. At around the same time, my dad sat me down for a talk. I think he could sense that the fighting was taking its toll on me. Maybe he felt guilty. And he told me a story.

My mom had been molested by her father when she was a child. When Nanny found out, she kicked him out and my mom hadn't seen him since. I was immediately empathetic towards her and realized she had been dealing with her own horrible childhood memories. As a young girl, my mom did not have the support systems and outlets she might have had today, and I can only imagine how this was one of the contributing factors to my mom's drinking; maybe she took some of the resentment she felt for her father out on my dad. After learning this family secret, it made sense why I'd never seen or heard of him. You know how in elementary school, they assign those family tree projects? Well, when I was in elementary school and had to make one, my dad (being the Navy vet and patriotic American that he was) always said, "Your other grandpa was a communist sympathizer, so he was killed." And we never spoke of him again.

In high school, I was one of the popular kids, liked by almost everyone. I had a cute cheerleader girlfriend and played on my high school baseball team. Baseball acted as my saving grace as I grew up. It gave me an outlet and reprieve from the struggles at home. I enjoyed playing with my friends; it kept my mind occupied and kept me in shape.

On the outside, I looked like the typical All-American kid, but I never let anyone get too close. I always hid the real me and the reality of my life. My typical high school day consisted of going to class during the day and going to baseball practice in the evening. I began bussing tables at night when I was fourteen. The money I earned from this job, I used to live the life of a normal teenager. I used my money for school lunches, going to the movies, and date nights with my girlfriend. I also paid for my own clothes and school supplies. I used my income to take care of my basic needs and spent a little extra from time to time so I could get out of the house and away from my parents. My routine meant that I could leave my house at 7:30 in the morning and get home at around 11 p.m.: anything to avoid spending too much time at home.

The reality of my life, however, meant that when the end of senior year came around, I knew all my friends would be moving forward but I would remain standing still. I developed a victim mindset that would eventually set me up to fail. This mindset made it all too easy for me to transition into severe depression and anxiety as a young adult. All it took was graduating high school, losing my friends, quitting baseball, and having my girlfriend move on to college without me. All of this triggered a steady downhill regression: I was in grave danger of repeating the cycle my parents had set before me.

CHAPTER 2

Rock Bottom and
a Mop Bucket

After graduating high school, many of my friends went on to college, but I remained stuck at home living with my parents. Like I mentioned, my parents never saved money for my college, and even if I could afford some of my tuition, they didn't have a dollar to contribute. It's a feeling that's hard to describe for me: most everyone I knew was going out into the world for bigger and brighter adventures, but I was left behind. Like a recurring nightmare where everyone is clambering to catch a boat to escape a scary zombie island but not everyone makes it off, I felt *trapped*. I saw the rescue boat take off without me.

This is when many of my bad decisions sprang up. I would have to overcome all these mistakes later. I began smoking at sixteen; by the time I finished high school, I was smoking a pack of cigarettes a day. I wasn't taking good care of my health or eating right. I didn't eat consistent meals, and what I did eat was usually fast food. I felt like a failure, I was depressed. This behavior carried on for the next two years, but I wasn't ready to give up on myself just yet. I had a part-time job at an insurance office answering phones and filing papers. I developed an interest in that particular field because I knew insurance agents could make really good money (as long as they passed an exam). During these two years, I attempted to take the exam twice but failed both times. I was frustrated and I could only watch as my dream of being a successful insurance agent faded to nothing. Without thinking, I quit my job at the insurance office. Now I was unemployed with no income. Naturally, it was the perfect time for me to land in debt.

My bank had given me a few credit cards, and of course I used them. I also had a recurring cell phone bill due each month, but I didn't understand anything about credit or how important it was. I was not credit responsible—in fact, I was downright reckless. My parents hadn't explained to me what credit was and how it could affect me long-term, and without a job to support me, I was unable to pay the minimum due on my credit cards. Eventually I stopped paying my cell phone bill too. I wasn't even twenty years old and I was already researching bankruptcy.

With failed exams, no job, and piling debt, I was at the lowest of lows. I felt that life had chewed me up and spat me back out. There were days I couldn't even leave my bedroom. I so badly wanted to quit. I didn't even have my parents' rundown car anymore. But here is where I'm certain God stepped in and sent people—angels—into my life. Everything would gradually begin to change, though I wouldn't see it just yet.

My aunt Cindi knew I needed some serious help, and fortunately, she had always been an angel in my life. She knew I needed to leave my parents' house, so she bought a twenty-year-old Honda Civic for me and encouraged me to move out by offering an alternative: that I go to Oregon and live with her daughter, my younger cousin Brittany, who was going off to college. She wanted to give me a fresh start, and said I could live there rent-free for a few months while I searched for a job. I didn't really want to go, but I knew there was nothing left for me at my parents' house, and I welcomed the new opportunity. At this point, I literally had nothing left to lose!

I crammed the Honda with every last one of my belongings, and headed to a new city in a new state. I knew no one apart from my cousin. Here I was, an unemployed, overweight heavy smoker, with bad credit and depression. I searched everywhere for a job: online, in-person, and door-to-door, yet I couldn't find anything. Many people weren't hiring, and of the places that were, I never heard back from. I filled out application after application, but to no avail—until I saw an ad in the paper about a sales position.

I went down to speak with the manager about the job. He was friendly and proceeded to ask me some basic interview questions. I confessed that even though I didn't have a sales background and very little work experience, I was a hard worker and a quick learner. The interview went well and he was open to giving me a chance, but his next statement had me frozen in my tracks: "Ok Ace, all we need to do now is perform a standard credit check." I asked him why they would need to check my credit. Well, *of course* it was necessary: I would be helping people finance purchases that required them to apply for credit, and I would be dealing with their personal, sensitive information. He informed me that the company had a "minimum credit score requirement" for the sales associates. My palms were sweaty, and all I could do was stare at my shoes. My childhood embarrassments and recent mistakes of my early adulthood flashed before me like a giant billboard. They all lead to one, obvious conclusion: "FAILURE!"

Of course, a few moments after the check, he gave me

a sympathetic look and told me he couldn't hire me because my credit score was a 400. He reassured me that I seemed like a nice guy and that, if I could get my credit score up, I could return to apply again. When he rose to shake my hand, I was too embarrassed to look him in the eye. Swallowing back my twenty years of shame, I thanked him. I was angry: I was angry at him and at that stupid policy. How could I pay off my debt without a job? How could I get a job with debt on my credit? I was in a no-win situation, stuck on a hamster wheel, running in endless circles. But when I finally allowed myself to look at the bigger picture, I knew the truth. I had no one to blame but myself. I had no one to be angry at but *myself*.

It was then that I was finally served a hardcore dose of reality. Walking along the downtown streets of this college town, I became aware of the homeless people in the streets. I stared at them as I walked by, with their dogs, their blankets, and their garbage bags filled with what little they owned. On any other day, I would have judged them as bad people—as criminals and drug addicts who had done something wrong to end up on the streets. Today, however, I saw them differently. Maybe they were at their wits' end, like I was. Maybe they had also sat through a shameful interview, like I had. Maybe they had finally decided to give up. I took a long, hard, honest look at them and told myself that any one of these individuals could have been me. Realistically, I wasn't all that far from living on the streets either.

Not long after the homeless encounter, I passed a small motel with a "help wanted" sign in the window. It was for a janitor. Now, I can honestly say that being a janitor was the *last* thing on my mind. I would have rather been literally *anything but* a janitor. Keep in mind, though, I had just experienced a sobering wake-up call. At this point, I just wanted a job—even if it was a janitor. I was still in a tailspin and feeling rather low from being denied a job based on my credit score; I didn't have a long resume of experience, and frankly, I had nothing else to offer but my hard work ethic. Why should I see myself as *too good* to be a janitor? I would be lucky if they gave me the position. I tucked my pride away, and went inside to inquire about the position.

The motel was a small, well-kept, inn-styled establishment that catered to out-of-towners who usually visited during the annual Shakespeare Festival. I went up to the front desk, mustered up a smile, and asked about the opening for a janitor. I was then directed to wait outside for the manager, a short, stocky guy with a pleasant demeanor. I introduced myself as we shook hands and began to inquire about the job. He stopped me before I could go on. The job would not be fun or easy, he explained. The position would involve cleaning up messes, vacuuming, scrubbing toilets, and other tedious tasks. I would be responsible for cleaning the motel—inside and out—and helping him with all maintenance and housekeeping tasks as needed, especially when the motel was understaffed. He reiterated the extent of cleaning and the mundanity of the job, and reminded me that the position paid minimum wage, which at the time was $6.00 per hour. When I told him that I understood and that I still wanted the position, the manager looked puzzled.

He had most certainly felt my desperation by the simple fact I was still standing there. He ended the interview with a simple question: "Why do you want the job?" But there was no simple answer. I couldn't get a job anywhere else, my credit was bad, I lacked experience and a college education—but I couldn't tell him that. I couldn't let my utter desperation show. Instead,

I explained that I had just relocated from California and was looking to start over in a new place. I admitted that I didn't have much experience, but that I was a good person and a hard worker. I told him that I'd be the best janitor he'd ever had. He laughed and said, "All right Ace, I'm going to give you a chance – you start tomorrow at 7:00 a.m."

So, there I was: still overweight, still smoking, and still depressed—only now I was making minimum wage; and here is where we find glimmers of the *overcomer's mindset* I referred to earlier. There was still a long road ahead, but I had taken the first crucial steps in the right direction. In the meantime, I continued living at my aunt's house with Brittany; the holidays were approaching and she was going home for Thanksgiving. I had to stay in Oregon partly because of work, but mostly because I couldn't afford to put gas in my engine. Brittany had asked me to place an ad online looking for a roommate—my aunt had a vacant third bedroom in need of occupancy. I posted the ad and someone replied right away: a Japanese international student who wanted to view the room over the weekend.

We arranged for Yuka to visit later that week so that I could show her around, only the greater part of her visit was spent simply talking in the kitchen. We talked for hours, and spoke about anything and everything. Yuka had grown up in Nagano, Japan with a regular upbringing. Like me, she had a sister, but unlike me, her childhood had not been so rocky. When I eventually opened up to her about my upbringing, she was surprised but not scared off. In fact, she would eventually become the love of my life. I called her the next day and asked her out. To my surprise, she said yes.

When we first started dating, the thing that struck me right away was that Yuka didn't drink alcohol. Coming from my own childhood experiences, this was music to my ears. Since we didn't have a lot of money, our dating life wasn't extravagant. We would usually just rent movies and watch them at home, and sometimes we would go out to eat. She exposed (or rather, forced) me to try many new dishes, like Thai food and curry, among other international cuisines I had never tasted before. I would always immediately say, "No I don't like it," and she would ask, "Have you ever tried it?" Of course I hadn't; I was just scared to try something new. She really coaxed me out of my shell and expanded my views regarding other cultures and foods. What a shift from sandwich bread hot dogs and fast food!

I had no idea what Yuka saw in an overweight smoker who was clearly depressed and deeply in debt. She might have seen potential in me, and I am so grateful that she did. She saw something in me that not even I could see. I needed her in my life and she arrived just in time; she loved me when I was at the lowest point in my life. Remember how, earlier in this narrative, I mentioned my certainty that God had stepped in and sent angels into my life? Yuka was another angel. By way of my aunt, God was lining up people who would forever change my life and my path.

With my new job and Yuka, things were finally beginning to look up for me. I wasn't so alone anymore. For the first time in my life, I was out on my own and gained a small sense of independence that I'd never felt before. Yet, I didn't feel happier. I was just a minimum wage janitor at a motel. I was over $8,000 in debt, and with a horrible credit score at that. I had no college degree. I drove a car that might as well have been a fossil, and lived paycheck to paycheck. Debt collectors were calling me on a daily basis and I only had $25 to my name. I was riddled with anxiety and depression. The love I felt for my girlfriend was overshadowed by the nagging thought that my life would never change.

It turns out that, in fantastic Ace fashion, my life was in fact about to get a bit more interesting. Surely by now you've grasped the fact I have some pretty snarky sarcasm about how life has treated me thus far. I lived in constant observation of Murphy's law: anything that *could* go wrong for the dapper young lad known as Ace Bowers, *would* go wrong. Oh boy (literally!) oh boy, were things about to swerve and hit me with a left hook I never saw coming. You know I love baseball, so let's put this portion of the story in a visual analogy to experience it the way I had.

curve·ball

noun

BASEBALL

1. a pitch thrown with a strong downward spin, causing the ball to drop suddenly and veer to the side as it approaches home plate.

When I was younger I would always ask my dad to teach me how to throw a curveball. After all, it's the best tool in a pitcher's arsenal and I wanted to master it. Despite my fervent pleas, my dad would always say I wasn't ready yet: when he finally decided I was, he'd teach me. Now in baseball, a great pitcher has a nasty curveball that is almost impossible to hit. Take a look at the definition: the ball is literally thrown with a strong downward spin, but then it veers off to the side as it reaches home plate before the batter can hit it. Done correctly, you're guaranteed a strike out almost every time. The spin and curve are what make it impossible to hit. Life was about to throw me a curveball, veering into a direction I just could not anticipate. Was I ready to hit it, or would I strike out? Here I was, taking baby steps to get my life in order, and now the game had changed again! It felt like I just couldn't catch a break.

I've always thought about how I would act in certain situations. What would I do if I was inside a bank and it was being robbed? What if I was on an airplane and it was about to crash? I always imagined how I would behave: would it be confidently and heroically? Or would I be overcome with fear and panic? In the end, you never really know how you will react unless, and until, you are living in that situation.

I was at work when I found out Yuka was pregnant. I had just finished my shift and I was walking to my car when I received the text message. All it said was: "I think I'm pregnant." Here's the wind up and the pitch... swing and a miss! *Had I just read that right?*

It took a couple seconds to hit, and as soon as it did, a wave of a thousand simultaneous thoughts and emotions came plummeting down on me. *Ah, there was that famous curveball I foretold.* It hit me right between the eyes and I had an instant panic attack. My palms were sweaty, and my mind flooded with thoughts—most of them of self-doubt and fear. No matter how I looked at it, I just couldn't find the silver lining to my circumstance. And I was angry—at myself! Because once again, I felt that I had unknowingly played into the same destructive cycle I had lived through as a child. *Oh God, was I going to end up like my parents?*

I sat in my car, frozen with disbelief. I was lost in the magnitude of my situation. I stayed there for what felt like hours; somehow, I zoned out, and when I came to, I realized I hadn't even replied to my girlfriend. Yuka had just told me something so personal, and I had left her waiting anxiously by her phone for my response. But how could I respond to *this*? It definitely didn't feel the way movies make it look—when a happy couple is on screen and the woman reveals some big news and they both jump up and down hugging each other and they proceed to tell one another that they love each other so much and *oh*, how excited they are! But this moment didn't feel like that at all. My thoughts should have been with Yuka and how she was feeling, but I was in shock. If we were watching the movie of my life, this would have been the moment the narrator says, "Man down, man down!"

Eventually, I did respond with, "Are you sure?" The skeptic in me insisted on reliable results before I gave in to any further panic. We wouldn't base our future on the inconsistency of a home pregnancy test. No, for something this important, we would visit a real doctor.

And it turned out our baby would be arriving in eight short months.

CHAPTER 3
The Noah Effect

There it was: my wakeup call. Those two words, "I'm pregnant," and the realization that I was going to be a father. But I had nothing to offer—I had gotten nowhere in life. The thought of becoming a minimum wage dad scared me to death. Would I put my child through worse than the adolescence I had endured? How much did diapers cost? How would we pay for the childbirth? The questions I asked myself were never-ending. Could I even afford to buy diapers, and if I couldn't, was I prepared to humble myself and ask for welfare? I was thousands of dollars in debt and currently working for minimum wage. I knew I couldn't support a family on this little income, and I was on my way to becoming yet another statistic of the poor and uneducated lower class. I felt life mocking me; the very life I had tried escaping as a child would become my reality. Would my blue-collar roots haunt me forever? I had promised myself I would break my family's cycle, not repeat it.

I sat in my car with these thoughts running through my mind for what seemed like hours. Eventually, I looked up and caught a glimpse of myself in the rear-view mirror: all I saw was a toilet cleaner with $25 in his bank account. I saw a man who had let himself go. A man about to unwittingly walk in his father's footsteps. Looking into that rear-view mirror was like looking back in time; all those painful memories swept over my conscious thoughts. I truly believe this was my lowest point.

It's a paralyzing realization to have just celebrated your 22nd birthday, to be broke, and to learn that you will be a father—I mean, I barely had enough energy to get out of bed in the morning, let alone raise a child! I found myself back at work, clutching my mop. I must have daydreamed again, occupied with the frightening thought that *this*—this life as a janitor—was in fact my life. I began mopping again but became transfixed by my reflection in the murky water I was using to wash the floors. It reminded me of my future: dark, bleak and unclear. Constantly hovering over me was the worry about how to handle the news I'd just been given. To some people, the news of fatherhood would be the happiest of their life, but to me, it was terrifying. I was entering a new chapter of my life that was uncertain, and I felt totally unprepared.

Oh, the changes I would have to make! Right up to this point, my biggest problems were about having enough money for gas and cigarettes. Then, a simple text, two words, life altering news, and a woman I loved on the other end waiting for my response. If I knew back then that everything would work out, maybe I would have mustered some happiness and relished the fact that hey, *I was gonna be a dad*! Instead my "glass half-empty" outlook coldly reminded me that I wasn't married, I wasn't ready, and I wasn't much of anything.

So as usual, I was feeling sorry for myself and allowing my mind to roam uncontrollably. But let's return to those two little words, "I'm pregnant!" Lest we forget, I was freaking out. It was normal for me to run a self-evaluation check at this point in my meltdown. Yuka and I were *bringing a child into the world*, so was I looking for an excuse to get out of being a daddy? No, but I *was* trying to decide if I was fit to even raise a child. Keep in mind, I didn't have much confidence in myself and I hadn't maintained a terrific track record as a responsible adult thus far. Would I be good enough for this baby, good enough for Yuka? Could I bring a child into an unhealthy environment? Because let's be honest, the way I was living *was* unhealthy.

People I knew at the time suggested we get an abortion, for a laundry list of reasons: we were barely 22, I made minimum wage, children are expensive... the list went on. The real point of their arguments was that Yuka and I wouldn't have a life. "What do you really know about raising a kid?" was another common theme. But there would be no talk of getting an abortion. Their advice went in one ear and out the other, and I would not entertain the thought. Something about this child felt as though it were meant to happen. No matter how bad off our situation was, we knew we were going to have this baby.

Many people don't have abortions due to their religious beliefs, but I want to preface this by stating that I am no *holier-than-thou* holy roller. I don't live as someone who openly practices faith. However, I do—and I have—always believed in God and that He has been with me at every point in my life. Yuka would not entertain the thought of an abortion on principle. I couldn't, not because of a religious condemnation of abortion, but because of a *feeling*. I believed that, with this child, God was testing me in some way; becoming a parent at this juncture in my life was *exactly* what I was meant to do. And it's true that without my newborn child, I would not be where I am today.

Even though I felt broken hearted, I felt inexplicably

closer to God. Maybe my inner spirit was crying out to God to deliver me from this minimum wage life of depression. He knew something I didn't: that I wouldn't be motivated to turn my life around alone. I grew to accept Yuka's news; over time, it frightened me less, and I came to understand that this had been a blessing from God. Looking back, I realize that He knew having a child was the *only* thing that might motivate me. Deep down, I knew it too. If you have a relationship with God or know someone who does, then I'm sure you've heard the saying, "It's in God's timing," and through my own experience, I came to witness this firsthand. For me, God's timing was *everything*. Had I gotten anyone pregnant while still living with my parents, the outcome would have been drastically different. The events that turned my life around following this news would not have taken place, and I would not be writing the memoir you are reading today. I truly believe that, being on my own, away from my parents and loving Yuka the way I did, forced me to dig deeper in search of a way to better myself.

Yuka was an international student finishing her senior year of college. After she graduated, her visa would expire, and she would have to return to Japan. What would this mean for us and our baby? I was thrown into an unfamiliar world filled with complicated decisions I had to make, with lifelong consequences. There were three of us now to consider, not just me, and we only had each other to figure everything out. I knew that I loved Yuka and wanted to eventually marry her, and since she was pregnant and would have to leave soon, I needed to do the right thing. We went down to the local city hall and we got married legally.

When our son came into the world, everything changed in the blink of an eye. I suggested "Noah," a name that immediately popped into my head at the prospect of having a son. This name spoke to me in particular, especially because I felt that his birth was God's blessing to me. I found a correlation between him and *Noah's Ark*, the biblical story I find the most kinship with. God had spared Noah, choosing him and his family and the world's animals, to start humanity over again. His flood purged and cleansed the Earth of man's evil, placing his trust into Noah's hands.

Just like Noah from the Book of Genesis, I was given a second chance and a new beginning with my son. Thanks to him, my outlook would slowly change for the better, and I would blossom into the man I was made to be. Noah saved me. God saved me. The title of this chapter, "The Noah Effect," is dedicated to this blessing. Noah became my motivation to do better: when Yuka first told me she was pregnant, I quit smoking *that same day*. Two months later, I began a diet and lost 85 pounds over the next four months. Noah is, truly, the reason for my transformation. Like the Genesis flood, I felt cleansed and renewed. I genuinely felt that God had lifted me from my pit of self-loathing and dejection and had given me the ultimate reason to succeed, to *capture* that overcomer's mindset. Had I listened to the people in my life, Noah wouldn't be here today, and I know I wouldn't be where I am today either.

CHAPTER 4
Footsteps into Fatherhood

I preface this chapter with the word *footsteps*. No one—no matter their experience—is ever fully ready to become a father. You have to learn mental, physical, and financial challenges as you go. And that's what I did: I took baby steps, footsteps, into fatherhood. Suddenly my life's purpose had new meaning; my kids would become the center of my universe and every waking breath I took would be dedicated to providing for and protecting them. I made a promise to myself that I would give everything I had to raising my kids right.

By now, you know that I'm about to become a father and that Yuka and I have married. Even though I had a newfound motivation named Noah, this was not going to be a walk in the park. I was still broke, and now, I had a budding family to care for. Of the millions of difficult decisions we had to make, at the forefront was how were we *ever* going to balance caring for Noah with our hectic lives? I was a working janitor, Yuka was still in school, we had very few friends and family in Oregon, and the costs of daycare were higher than my income.

All of my family lived in California and all of her family

lived in Japan, but my parents said they would let us live with them for a year, to save as much money as we could. I had one year, and *only* one year, to save as much as possible for a down payment on a house.

So, I quit my job as a janitor at the motel, Yuka completed school, we packed our life into a U-Haul truck and drove from Oregon to California. This was the first time that Yuka would ever meet my whole family and see my house. That damn house, haunted with memories. To say I was nervous would be the understatement of the century! Stepping back into that environment after two years away was an immense shock for me. I was immediately drowned by old memories—of the fights. But now it wouldn't be just me who was affected: my wife and son would be there for me to literally hand down the lifestyle I had inherited. I refused to allow my family to endure what I had. Staying longer than a year was not an option.

Now I was unemployed—again, and living with my parents—again. Was I all the way back at square one? No. This time, I had a wife and son that I was responsible for, and I had made up my mind: I wouldn't fail them. I'd have to hustle and work harder than I'd ever worked before, but I was going to make this happen! My life *would* change for the better. But with everything said and done, I am profoundly grateful to my parents for allowing us to move in with them when Noah was born. Though they put me through a lot as a child, they really came through for me when I needed them most. Without them, we wouldn't have been able to get a head start on our savings for our family. I will always be thankful to them.

In the time that passed between Yuka announcing her pregnancy and Noah's birth, I finally found the drive to pull my act together. In a later chapter, I'll explain in detail the hustle

ears. But for
er Noah, we
ths later: our
my life when
s hustling my
tablished and
I made great

y prioritizing
ing them my
ntal behavior
ment. So, my
ent to giving
of them a kiss
ms before bed
from my own
h to me, as it
eat dinner as
eir day. Yuka
balanced, so
a harmonious
ent; she is no
ile I am more
well-rounded

ally watching
We even play
cause we want
ow that. Above
matter what is
overshadowed

by our problems. Gro

cast aside over my par

swept under the rug in

unmoored during most

myself that I'd never le

to know that they can t

    At an early age,

how important it is to

being respectful and ha

know how they treat tH

treat other people. I als

Noah and Ariel watch

that observing me in ho

handle relationships in t

for me as a father to g

growing up, and I kno

instill. I want to shelter

exposed to, from things

don't want to shelter th

for the real world. I war

expose them to diverse

them to explore and try

the choices I never had.

    As difficult as my

me into the dad I am

parent's actions and ho

on the forefront of my mi

memories growing up th

I want my kids to be k

can, from traveling and

travel as often as we can

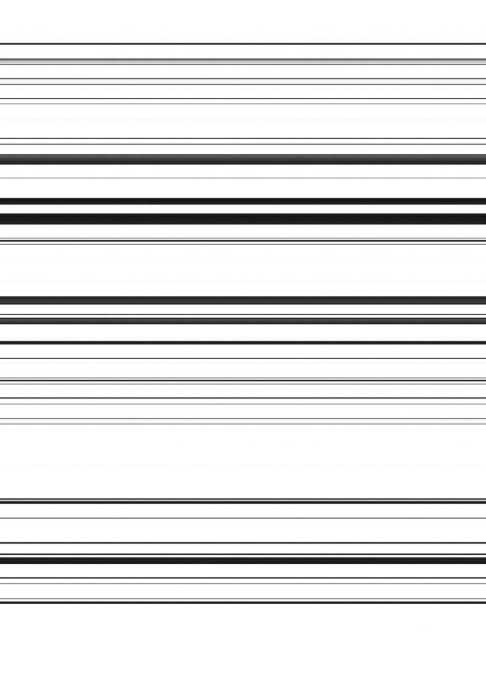

CHAPTER 4
Footsteps into Fatherhood

I preface this chapter with the word *footsteps*. No one—no matter their experience—is ever fully ready to become a father. You have to learn mental, physical, and financial challenges as you go. And that's what I did: I took baby steps, footsteps, into fatherhood. Suddenly my life's purpose had new meaning; my kids would become the center of my universe and every waking breath I took would be dedicated to providing for and protecting them. I made a promise to myself that I would give everything I had to raising my kids right.

By now, you know that I'm about to become a father and that Yuka and I have married. Even though I had a newfound motivation named Noah, this was not going to be a walk in the park. I was still broke, and now, I had a budding family to care for. Of the millions of difficult decisions we had to make, at the forefront was how were we *ever* going to balance caring for Noah with our hectic lives? I was a working janitor, Yuka was still in school, we had very few friends and family in Oregon, and the costs of daycare were higher than my income.

All of my family lived in California and all of her family

lived in Japan, but my parents said they would let us live with them for a year, to save as much money as we could. I had one year, and *only* one year, to save as much as possible for a down payment on a house.

So, I quit my job as a janitor at the motel, Yuka completed school, we packed our life into a U-Haul truck and drove from Oregon to California. This was the first time that Yuka would ever meet my whole family and see my house. That damn house, haunted with memories. To say I was nervous would be the understatement of the century! Stepping back into that environment after two years away was an immense shock for me. I was immediately drowned by old memories—of the fights. But now it wouldn't be just me who was affected: my wife and son would be there for me to literally hand down the lifestyle I had inherited. I refused to allow my family to endure what I had. Staying longer than a year was not an option.

Now I was unemployed—again, and living with my parents—again. Was I all the way back at square one? No. This time, I had a wife and son that I was responsible for, and I had made up my mind: I wouldn't fail them. I'd have to hustle and work harder than I'd ever worked before, but I was going to make this happen! My life *would* change for the better. But with everything said and done, I am profoundly grateful to my parents for allowing us to move in with them when Noah was born. Though they put me through a lot as a child, they really came through for me when I needed them most. Without them, we wouldn't have been able to get a head start on our savings for our family. I will always be thankful to them.

In the time that passed between Yuka announcing her pregnancy and Noah's birth, I finally found the drive to pull my act together. In a later chapter, I'll explain in detail the hustle it took to get my career off the ground in those years. But for now, let's jump ahead a bit into fatherhood. After Noah, we had a second addition to our family eighteen months later: our daughter, Ariel. I was at two very different points in my life when I had each of my kids. When Noah was born, I was hustling my ass off. When Ariel was born, I was a bit more established and we had our own house. Importantly, in that time, I made great efforts to be the best father I could.

I make sure my kids know I love them by prioritizing the time I spend with them and openly showing them my affection. I realized from my childhood that parental behavior is tremendously influential to a child's development. So, my life revolves around my children and my commitment to giving them the best childhood I can. At night I give each of them a kiss no matter what, and sometimes I stop by their rooms before bed to cuddle and have story time. This I picked up from my own mom and dad: our bedtime routine meant so much to me, as it does for Noah and Ariel now. We try to regularly eat dinner as a family, and I use that time to ask them about their day. Yuka and I are a good fit for parenting together. We're balanced, so it's easy to combine our parenting skills to create a harmonious environment for our kids. Yuka is the strict parent; she is no nonsense when it comes to academics. Meanwhile I am more easygoing; I want my kids to grow into good, well-rounded individuals.

We spend time with them every Sunday, usually watching movies, making popcorn, and playing games. We even play chess or card games a couple of times a week, because we want to be involved in their lives and for them to know that. Above all, I want Noah and Ariel to understand that, no matter what is going on in my life or in Yuka's, they will *never* be overshadowed by our problems. Growing up, my siblings and I were quickly cast aside over my parents' issues. Feelings and honesty were swept under the rug in favor of tense silence. I felt forgotten and unmoored during most of my childhood as a result. I promised myself that I'd never let that happen again. I want my children to know that they can talk to me.

At an early age, I taught them the value of a dollar and how important it is to work hard. I stressed the importance of being respectful and having a good attitude. I wanted them to know how they treat their mom and dad will affect how they treat other people. I also try and set a good example, because Noah and Ariel watch Yuka and me like little hawks. I know that observing me in how I treat their mom will affect how they handle relationships in the future. But the most important thing for me as a father to give my kids, is *balance*. I didn't have it growing up, and I know the kind of anxiety that instability can instill. I want to shelter my kids from the painful events I was exposed to, from things they're too young to learn, but I also don't want to shelter them so much that they feel unprepared for the real world. I want to give them the tools to succeed and expose them to diverse thinking, different cultures, and allow them to explore and try things for themselves. I am giving them the choices I never had.

As difficult as my childhood was for me, I think it shaped me into the dad I am today. Understanding the weight of a parent's actions and how it impacts his or her children is always on the forefront of my mind. I don't want my kids to have painful memories growing up that could alter the course of their lives. I want my kids to be *kids*, and to experience everything they can, from traveling and playing sports, to art and culture. We travel as often as we can to allow Noah and Ariel to experience the many sides of life. Having a multicultural household has motivated us to expose our children to Japanese culture and implement traditional Japanese holidays into our home.

Yuka enriched my life tenfold when she introduced me to new foods and lifestyles I hadn't tried before, so I strive to do the same for my kids. I want them to try things I was never able to as a kid. Seeing them ski and snowboard in the winter brings me staggering joy, because I never had the chance to try those activities myself growing up! I love having new adventures and going new places with them. Seeing the smiles on their faces and being a part of their happiness allows me to get a part of my childhood back.

My relationship with each of my kids is very different. While the lessons and time I give each of them are equal, the way we bond and spend one-on-one time together is very different. You know why Noah is named Noah, but let me tell you the story behind my daughter's name. Ariel means *lion of God*, and she certainly lives up to that title (in fact, several of her teachers have told me she is the "alpha" in her class). When she was born, Noah would try to say her name, but he must have struggled with those consonants, because it always came out as "YaYa." It became her nickname from that moment on.

Ariel is opinionated, direct, and not afraid to tell it like it is. I love that about her. I often tell her she's going to be the CEO of a big company one day. Personality-wise, she's Noah's total opposite. Noah is reserved and introverted with his expressions. He is like me in that respect: I remember, on Noah's eighth birthday we were dining out and he ordered a burger and fries with a side of apples. The food was delivered but they had forgotten his apples. When the waitress came back to check on us, she asked if everything was ok. My son, the cordial young man, did not call attention to this mistake. However, my daughter pointed out (quite fiercely!) to the waitress she had forgotten her brother's apples. She also made it *extremely* clear that it was his birthday.

Ariel and I share a very unique connection and many of the same interests. We both love cars. She can tell you the difference between American muscle and other classic sports cars. She also loves music as much as I do. My favorite singer is Frank Sinatra and her favorite song is "I've Got You Under My Skin." When his songs come on the radio, she and I sing them together. Of course she knows every word. I see so much of myself in Ariel. Noah reminds me more of his mother because of his engineering mindset. They often see things in black and white. Ariel picks up on the gray areas of life like I do. She has a more abstract vision that will allow her more flexibility as she grows older.

Noah and I bonded through baseball, much like how my dad and I did when I was younger. He always viewed baseball as America's pastime and a crucial element of American culture. That was one of the best things my father did for me, and I cherished those memories. It's something of a tradition in my family which has tied three generations together: my dad's father taught him about baseball, my dad taught me, and now I teach my son. I've coached Noah's baseball team for six years now. I was there since the very beginning during his first year playing, when he was just five years old. My dad, who lives out in the countryside now, has driven over two hours just to come to Noah's baseball games.

If there's anyone that loves my kids more than me, it has to be my mom and dad—their "Nana" and "Papa," as they like to call them. Papa treasures his time with them. Every summer he looks forward to them spending a few weeks on the family farm he was able to acquire on a VA loan a few years back. They collect the eggs from the hens in the morning and my mom cooks them for breakfast. My dad has all his equipment from his days as a machinist in his garage. Noah, having an engineer's mindset, loves to spend time with Papa learning how to use all of those machines.

I took my family to Disneyland in 2013. Since the crushing blow I had felt during my own childhood trip from my mother's meltdown, I wanted to finally have the resort trip of my dreams. With my wife and children, I was able to provide the experience for them that I had so dearly missed. Seeing the looks on their faces and the fun they had, I accomplished my childhood dream. I spared no expenses and we stayed in the Disneyland Hotel. This memory remains my proudest accomplishment as a father. My kids enjoyed it, probably not as much as I did, but being there with them seemed like my life had come full circle.

CHAPTER 5
Millionaire Moves

One of the most beneficial things my father taught me as a child was how to play baseball. Not only did it teach me strategic principles I would later use in life, but I also loved spending that time with him. My dad taught me one of the most important fundamentals of the game, which is that home runs are not the most important thing when stepping up to the plate. Base hits were the main objective; actually getting on base was critical to scoring. This was achieved through small, yet consistent progress: it is the key to winning. This basic principle can be applied all throughout life but especially in your career, by learning to move forward in business or at work with small, significant steps, making progress each time. I want to show you in this chapter how I applied the principles of baseball to my life and turned them into millionaire moves.

Even though my childhood was painful at times, it gave me the chance to develop some unique skills. Maturing at a young age in that type of environment, I became highly intuitive. I was very socially aware and developed skills that allowed me to read people accurately. I quickly learned how to read a room.

Growing up, I didn't have a choice. I had to learn how to navigate my parents' emotional landmines to survive. I needed to be able to walk into a room and immediately discern the mood, so I observed people, not only by what they would say, but through their body language and nonverbal communication. As a result, I could easily adapt my personality to get along well with others by recognizing their silent thoughts and empathizing with them. And so I honed in on this skill set. I didn't need to learn them, but rather, strengthened them until they became invaluable elements of my personality and propelled me towards success.

You always hear the phrase, "Communication is key," and that's true. I value communication and my ability to interact and talk to people on different levels. You need to be flexible, capable of acclimating to various circumstances and unexpected change. Couple that with the ability to easily adjust to others and it's a valuable, priceless tool in today's business world. This would become one of my greatest strengths later on in my career.

Looking back, I realize I made some serious mistakes growing up that led to my own self-destructive behavior. In my mind, I was always feeling sorry for myself and ashamed of my family. This thinking led to the development of a massive chip on my shoulder: the more embarrassed my family made me, the bigger the chip became. I lived under the assumption that all my friends had it so much better than I did, and my unstable environment only further fueled my self-pity. If I wanted to grow into a better person, the first move I needed to make was *overcoming this mindset*. Mindset is *everything*. Endlessly complaining about what I didn't have would get me nowhere; instead I had to start going after what I wanted. Of course, this was a task easier said than done, and it can be incredibly overwhelming when you're faced with so much to change about yourself. It's just as easy to quit while you're ahead.

I tackled what I had direct control over first: my unhealthy habits. All it took was discipline and a determined mindset, and over time as my confidence increased, I realized that I had control over many more facets of my life. All these things built momentum which allowed me to accomplish the rest of my goals from then on. Not only should you keep a positive mindset in attempting to alter your lifestyle, but you *must* stay open-minded. Mindset is a key component in your pursuit of success, for it is essentially the way you perceive yourself and your current circumstances. Motivation is everything.

To make sincere millionaire moves, you *must* be motivated. You cannot rely on others to motivate you—rather, find a means to *discover* your own motivation. One of the biggest ways I found mine was by using the very thing that hurt me in the first place. When I found out I was going to have a baby, my painful childhood recollections came rushing back. They crushed me with misery, embarrassment, and shame. And in that moment, I knew I never wanted my child to experience the pain I had endured. Instead of dwelling in pity all over again, I made my past work *for* me, not against me. I used every last biting memory as motivation to fuel my endeavors and inspire me to create a better plan for my family's future. I had found my reason to succeed: it was my child, in the family I was building with Yuka, and in my need to reap some benefit from my unpleasant past.

After I adjusted my mindset and found my motivation, I needed to tie everything together with goals and a plan. I had short-term goals—things I needed to do right away—and some long-term goals that demanded I work my ass off. I also had to face many past failures: sometimes we fail at something and give up. We often abandon that goal, either out of fear, or out of frustration. If I was going to put my best foot forward, I would have to acknowledge my mistakes, one way or another.

So, the *instant* I found out that Yuka was pregnant with Noah, I quit smoking. I had previously attempted to stop smoking, but it wasn't until I was sparked by the news of becoming a father that I finally quit for good. There was no patch, no gum, no magic pill, but rather the willpower and determination to be the kind of father I wanted my child to have. I made up my mind: it had to stop *now*. There were two reasons this was important: first, because I had made it a habit to purchase a pack a day, and I couldn't afford to waste money on nonsense. Second, because smoking was bad for me, it would be bad for the baby, and I needed to be my strongest self to raise this child.

The next thing I needed to do was lose weight. I was very heavy for my size, at 5'10" and 230 pounds. My knees hurt daily, and walking upstairs to my apartment made me winded. I never exercised—I had when I played sports in school, but that wasn't on purpose. I hated exercise and frankly, I never had time for it. I wanted to lose weight but I didn't know how: I didn't know what calories were, much less what to read on food labels. I saw food as a friend. It would comfort me during bad times and good times, and it made me happy.

I had to change the way I looked at food—I should eat to live, not live to eat. I know that sounds cliché, but it's true. I needed to be mindful of what I was eating, especially since I didn't like to exercise. I learned to count calories and forced myself to drink only water. This was all part of my plan to get healthy. I didn't feel good, and if I didn't feel good, it would be too hard to stay motivated. Getting healthy not for vanity, but to reach a place where I felt good, took me farther than I expected. When all was said and done, with my new mindset, I was able to lose 85 pounds in four months.

You must first develop a plan, something to work towards. My goal was to save money, make a six-figure income, and build wealth for me and my family. I didn't want my kids to know what it felt like to be poor, and in order for me to do that, I had to stay committed to my goals and uphold a strong work ethic. Lazy people will never succeed, and in order to work towards the life I envisioned for my family, I couldn't be afraid of hard work. No matter where I was employed, I had two rules of thumb that I always followed: first, I made it a habit to know more than I needed to know and to take the initiative to learn anything that could help me succeed on my own. Second, I always did more than what I was paid to do. I volunteered for projects and took on extra loads. I often worked two jobs for extra income and experience. My efforts helped me stand out as a great collaborator and a valuable part of the team.

This drive led me through a series of employers, wherein I never settled and defiantly propelled myself to do more than was expected. This journey began with me as a lackluster janitor. When Yuka and I moved in with my parents, I started working as an "on call" security guard, ready to fill in for any shift, at any time. This included holidays and graveyard shifts. While making $12 per hour at this job, I was also studying for my insurance exam. In the second chapter of this book, I mentioned my attempts—and failures—at becoming an insurance broker, before subsequently giving up. This was my third attempt. Quitting this goal had never sat well with me, and now it was time to face my failures head on. But this time around, I was not alone. I had Yuka. She helped me study and after tirelessly poring over textbooks and flashcards together for a month, I finally passed in 2007. I could now sell insurance while still maintaining my position as a security guard.

Whenever I wasn't scheduled to work a security guard shift, I would throw on a tie and sell insurance door to door, cold calling people. I visited small used car dealerships to leave my name in case anyone was buying a car and needed insurance, asking that they call me. And they did call me. A lot. Selling insurance became a tremendous source of income for me. I was making good money as an insurance agent, and I could have stopped hustling right there to live comfortably. But I didn't.

I would not allow pride to get in the way of providing for my family. Even though I already had two jobs, I refused to be complacent. I flipped cars and painted houses with my brother (who now worked as a house painter) on weekends. We could paint an entire house in a day or two, and he would compensate me in cash. I bought cars that needed work, negotiated a discount, repaired them, and then sold them for a profit. And so, I managed to save a lot of money and began to pay off my debt and repair my credit. After about a year of nonstop hard work, we bought a starter house with the help of a loan from Yuka's parents. The financial crisis of 2008 had made it almost impossible to get a bank loan, and with my credit in disrepair and all the side jobs that paid in cash, I knew getting a loan was out of the question. We paid our mortgage to Yuka's parents, instead of to the bank.

After about a year of working as a security guard, I was promoted to security guard supervisor at a Silicon Valley tech company called TiVo. I was now making $15 per hour. By this time, I had saved enough money to start investing in stocks, and by 2010, I got an entry-level job at that same company as a manual software quality assurance (QA) tester.

My security boss knew I was destined for greater things, and she often told me that I could, and *should*, be doing so much more than working as a security guard. She even encouraged me to explore something inside of TiVo if I could; she said that she would support me 100%, even if it meant losing me. It followed that the QA director at TiVo became the first person to give me the chance at entering the tech industry. Being a manual QA software tester was the lowest position at the entire company. It paid a mere $16 per hour—a dollar more than my security job, but that's all I needed. If I could get my foot in the door, I would let my work ethic, attitude, and personality speak for themselves.

To this day, I still remember that my interview was at 3:00 p.m. and that I ended my security shift at exactly 3:00 p.m. I closed up the security office and rushed down the hall to one of the meeting rooms where the director and a member of her team were waiting for me. I was so nervous and even apologized to them for the fact that I was still wearing my security guard uniform. But I passed the interview and got the job.

When I made the transition from security guard to low-level software tester, I learned that the tech industry, in general, lacked people with great social skills and personality. I realized then that my personality and ability to communicate well could take me very far. I learned as much as I could about software, and though I didn't learn to code (I didn't want to be a programmer), I took a class on coding for beginners. I knew that if I wanted to work closely with engineers one day, I would need to know the basics of coding and how to think like a programmer to communicate better with them. I read books at night about building software, testing software, and software processes, which helped me in my career immensely. I took it one step further, and went to night school to become certified in QA software testing. I worked all day and went to school all night, but I finished at the top of my class. I must have made an impression, because about a year later they asked me to come back and teach the class.

I worked at TiVo as a software QA tester for about a year. I now had a year of software testing under my belt, and as an added bonus, a QA certification after five months of night school. I was eventually hired as a contractor inside of Yahoo for a job that paid $36 per hour. Keep in mind, I was still flipping cars and investing in stocks. By the end of 2011, I was making some pretty good money and was ready to sell our starter home. Noah would soon be going to school, and I wanted to buy a home in a better neighborhood with a better school district.

While I was at Yahoo, an agency contacted me to do QA at Google. This was the chance of a lifetime for me. Google was a matchless opportunity and I would take full advantage and learn everything I could from the Ivy Leaguers around me.

I will never forget the day I interviewed: it was my first time ever stepping foot onto the Google campus. I was scheduled to have an interview with a few of the engineers and would meet my soon-to-be boss shortly after. He was the type who didn't mince his words, who held extremely high performance standards. His motto: "If you're comfortable, you're not growing." Fortunately, I passed the interview with him as well, and was offered the job. The team later told me that I had competed with, and beat out, almost *fifty* other candidates for that one opening! I worked at Google as a contractor, not a direct employee—but realistically, it was hard for me to see any difference between the two, other than the color of our ID badges.

Over the next six years at Google, I quickly learned that

most employees didn't last under my boss's management style because he demanded and expected excellence at all times. Under his leadership, everything was to be *perfect*, and the high workloads he delegated were to be fulfilled without a hitch. He had extremely high performance standards and would routinely push you to your breaking point—*but*, if you managed to pull through and come out the other end, you would have learned and grown exponentially.

Working for him, I dealt with several different employees with varying, incongruous agendas, who all communicated differently. From the first day on the job, I was expected to know everyone's agenda and expectations, and resolve any conflicts that arose. The task was easily overwhelming, but fortunately, my aptitude for communication got me through it. The discipline I developed had certainly helped, as well as the plain truth that I simply wouldn't *quit*. Yet, for one reason or another, many of my previous colleagues never came out the other end. After working with my boss for a year or so, he once said to me: "You've got something special in your personality and a work ethic that is hard to find. I need more people like you, Ace." That was high praise, coming from him!

The time I spent inside Google ultimately gave rise to two new valuable perspectives. I learned to spot truly intelligent and helpful people in a crowd, and I came to appreciate *humble intelligence*. In Silicon Valley, smart people are common, but it's the ones with *humility* to look out for—they are exceedingly rare, but unbelievably valuable. After reflecting on my years at Google, I realized that it's not the products, the free meals, or the perks that were important. Ultimately, it's the people you work with everyday who matter. The skills I would acquire and the knowledge I would consume encompass some of the most beneficial things I've learned throughout my career. I'm grateful for my time at Google; I literally worked side by side with some of the most brilliant people in the world. Everyone I worked with had that fancy education I had dreamed of, from universities I never had a chance to attend. But collaborating with these brilliant employees felt as though I had attended a Harvard, a Brown, or a Yale myself.

I wasn't quite a millionaire yet, but I was well on my way. I continued making millionaire moves, and never became comfortable with what I was earning, comfortable as my salary may have been. Yuka and I sold our first house for around $500,000. With our household income, I could get a loan from the bank for around $600,000. This gave me the purchasing power of roughly a million dollars to buy a home. Now, I could have bought a few properties outside Silicon Valley, or a million dollar home within Silicon Valley. If I bought multiple homes, I could live in one and rent the others for additional income, but after a lot of research, and following my gut instinct, I purchased a home near the new Apple headquarters in Cupertino. Even though I had paid a million dollars for that home, it turned out to be the best investment I had ever made.

During my six-year tenure at Google, I left for one year to work at a cybersecurity startup company in Cupertino called Bromium Inc. They offered me more than what I was currently making, namely a salary of $100,000 per year. This marked the first time in my life that I had ever earned a six-figure income, and the feeling that came with it was monumental! Working at Bromium came with unbelievable perks: I was even lucky enough to meet Robert Herjavec—yes, that same one from *Shark Tank* and a big investor in the company. I still own equity in that startup. I have thousands of shares; if they ever go public or are acquired, I'll receive a payout. The accumulation of my passive wealth from real estate and stocks, combined with my salary made my net worth a little over a million dollars. At just 28 years old, I became worth a million dollars. Five years prior, I had been making minimum wage as a janitor.

I remained at the startup for a little over a year, until my previous boss at Google contacted me to be his right-hand Senior QA manager for a new startup embedded within the firm. He needed someone like me for the startup, and offered me a salary of $125,000 annually, plus bonuses and equity. I jumped at the offer and worked at this company for about three years until it was acquired by a large investment firm in 2017. Once the acquisition was complete, I received a check in the mail for all of my shares of stock. With my million-dollar acquisition just four years earlier, and combined with all my new investments, stocks, and real estate, this profit effectively doubled my net worth. I was now a multi-millionaire at 32 years old.

CHAPTER 6
My Rock
(Kokoro no sasae)

When people think about falling in love, they often assume they're looking for their soulmate. There's nothing wrong with that, but *soulmate* has a fairytale-like connotation that can be hard to live up to, especially when the reality of life knocks you down. Sometimes people refer to their spouse or mate as their partner, better half, or companion. I think partner is the operative term, because the very definition of partner is *teammate*. When you're going through all the challenges of life, it is a far lighter load to take on when you have someone to share it with. I refer to my wife as my rock, or in Japanese, *kokoro no sasae*.

As I mentioned before, I was at a very low point in my life when I met my future wife. I had nothing to offer her but my love. She saw past my current situation—my state as a minimum wage janitor, utterly unestablished, and very much in debt. She had to have known life with me would not be glamorous or easy, but she still took a chance and loved me. That spoke volumes to me about her character. I felt safe enough to fully trust her.

Yuka had a very different upbringing from me. She lived

a typical, sheltered childhood; growing up, her focus was 100% academic. She wasn't forced to grow up and mature as quickly as I had been; she hadn't witnessed abuse or lived in poverty. Her parents were very concerned with her education and as a result, Yuka was always the star pupil with the best grades. When I met her, she was earning her degree in biology and chemistry. It's a miracle she even *considered* loving a guy with no formal education and enough emotional baggage to fill an airport. She always listened as I told her about everything from my past. Clearly it didn't scare her off, because we're still happily married to this day!

I look back and wish I could have offered Yuka a special wedding and filled her day with all the things little girls dream about when they get married, but we just couldn't afford it. Though she never expressed that she wanted a fairytale wedding—with a beautiful venue, matchless dress, and everything else to make it grand and unforgettable—in my heart, I know it's what she deserved. I wanted her parents to be there, but they were an ocean away. I thought to myself that we should at least share this special day with *some* family. I remember calling my mom a week before we got married and asking her and my dad to please drive up to Oregon. It was a six-hour drive from their house.

I really wanted them to be there when we were married. I wanted them to meet my new wife and their future daughter-in-law. *For goodness sakes*, she was carrying their grandchild! They told me that they didn't have the gas money to drive up there, that my dad couldn't afford to take a day off from work. I was sad, but I had come to expect these kinds of let downs in my life—this was nothing new to me. I compartmentalized this news like I did with every other disappointing or painful thing in my life, and moved on.

No matter what, I couldn't let my frustrated or saddened demeanor reflect onto Yuka; I worried she was witnessing firsthand the disappointments I had been through. I mean, what kind of family misses their own son's wedding? It didn't seem to bother her because she never said anything to me about it, ever. Thankfully, when Yuka *did* meet my parents for the first time as we unpacked our U-Haul back in California, they hit it off. My dad often tells me that she's his favorite person in the entire family. It could be because they share a very similar style of thinking, but I never really could figure out why they got along so well! Needless to say, he loves Yuka and she adores him right back.

Her personality is very even-keel and stable. This chapter is titled "My Rock" because, against all odds, Yuka remains unbelievably calm and balanced. Just like her daughter, she tells it like it is. And growing up as reserved as I did, where every battle and every issue was internal, her resolution to be so honest about her feelings was like a breath of fresh air. I was attracted to that because I didn't know what was missing from my life before I met her was this *truthfulness*, this sense of *balance*. She was so unlike my mother, the other female role model in my life. To see a woman so self-sufficient, so hardworking and so easy-going was unbelievably uplifting.

Yuka is an irreplaceable force in my life, and from the moment we met, what she has done for me has been nothing short of incredible. Life for us in the beginning was far from ideal. The deck was stacked against us, but she never wavered in her love for me, and more importantly, she never lost faith in me. My deep love and respect for her is ingrained in the fact that she has taken each leap of faith *with* me, hand in hand. I was like her box of chocolates: she had no *idea* what she was getting into, and still, she remained by my side. Her even-keeled nature and calm spirit would steady my rockiest days; I somehow knew I wouldn't fail, because I could feel her supportive spirit right beside me. Knowing she had the confidence in my ability to support us and our family carried me through some of the hardest times as a man trying to find his way. I *wanted* to succeed. Not for me, but for our kids. For *her*.

I remember that after Noah was born, all I wanted to do was stay by Yuka's side at the hospital. For a change, I wanted to show my love and support for *her*. But being the kind-hearted person she is, she was more worried about me going home to get some sleep, knowing I couldn't sleep anywhere but my own bed. I thought to myself, *this woman just gave birth to our son and she's worried about me!*

Now, before I have you gushing about Yuka and thinking she's this soft, sweet and oh-so fragile little woman... let me tell you about the birth of our second child. She woke me up at 3 a.m. and we rushed out to the hospital. I dropped her off at the entrance and hurried off to find a parking spot. In the short span of time it had taken me to park the car, run into the hospital, and find the room, Yuka had already given birth to our daughter. No epidural, no doctor, and no one by her side, just Yuka and her determination. We left the hospital a day later, Yuka marching out, her newborn daughter in one arm and her bags in the other. I thought to myself, my wife is a legit badass! (And then I rushed over to help her carry everything).

Yuka loves to cook and she's fantastic at it. I always joke and tell her that the only reason I married her was for her cooking. She likes to tease me with the notion that I was like a lost puppy when she found me. The truth is, I married her because I had never met someone as resilient, as truthful, as steady, as Yuka.

CHAPTER 7
Band of Brothers:
A tale of two roads

This chapter is dedicated to my closest friends, Anthony and Abe. They are my best friends, but more than that, they were the brothers I never had. They helped fill the hole in my heart left by my real brother who was never there. "Band of Brothers," the title of this chapter, is a play on words because I consider these guys family, but more than that, you may recognize this title from the 2001 HBO series. I bonded with both of them individually, over one TV show, and our friendships felt so special. Anthony introduced me to the show when we were teenagers, and we watched it together. He used to tell me that if he ever went to battle, he wanted me by his side in the foxhole because he knew I'd always have his back. It meant the world to me that someone trusted and thought of me like that.

A few years later, I shared *Band of Brothers* with Abe because of his love of the military. He had just returned from Texas where he was attending a military academy. We were around eighteen and had been contemplating joining the military. Even though I went to the recruiter's office and took the exam, it was Abe who ultimately enlisted, conveying that he had joined for both of us. To this day, this sentiment touches my heart. That's probably why he is Noah's godfather.

Let me slow down and back up; I want to share with you how special and different each of these guys were to me in my life. I met both of them in junior high school. Anthony and I were the same age and Abe was a year younger. While Abe and Anthony were my best friends, they weren't friends with each other. They were acquainted but hung out in completely different circles. Fortunately, I had a crossover personality, where I could fit in with anyone, so I just happened to be in each of their circles.

Let me first tell you about Anthony. Everybody chooses a bad path in life at some point: a bad decision, a temporary lapse in judgment, or a bout of depression. Most of us find our way back, but there are those who can't see the light at the end of the tunnel. They have *so much* potential but for one reason or another, can't stop themselves from going down the wrong path, until it becomes so familiar, they can't escape. Unfortunately, this happened to Anthony.

Anthony was the very first friend I made when we moved to Cupertino; he lived just down the street from me. He had a big heart and a larger-than-life personality. We shared a love for skateboarding, always had great conversations, and spent much of our time together. Anthony was the type of friend you could tell anything to and know with absolute certainty that he would listen, and never judge. He was one of the few friends I had where I felt completely comfortable sharing some of what I so often kept hidden behind my walls. Needless to say, we had been through some challenges together. His parents were divorced; I was there for him if he needed to talk, and he was there for me. It was hard for me to open up when I was younger, though given the imbalance and hardships I faced alone at home, I should have reached out more. One day, while spending the night at Anthony's house, I was inexplicably overwhelmed with sudden dread, panic, and the unspeakable need to escape. Panic set in. It was a full blown anxiety attack, my very first one. He saw me through that.

I was sixteen years old when 9/11 happened. I remember waking up to my phone ringing: it was Anthony calling to tell me that we had just been attacked. He said "Ace, man, wake up and turn on your TV!" And we sat there, each of us holding the phone, watching in silence. I gave him a ride to school like I did most days, and that morning, we did what we always did: had one of our deep talks. The focus that morning had shifted to current events and his aunt who worked at the World Trade Center. We contemplated both joining the military and how we would be supportive of one another if we went. It was a somber ride to school, two teenagers talking about innocent people dying.

We remained close throughout high school, though our paths grew further apart, and we later separated into different groups. Sadly, Anthony would eventually make the mistake of getting into drugs. Though many high schoolers smoked pot (even I had tried it a few times, but stayed uninterested), he quickly outgrew marijuana. He surrounded himself with the druggie crowd, and I had to watch as he fell deeper down a rabbit hole, chasing one high after the next. Mushrooms, acid, cocaine and ecstasy; he cycled through them all.

In spite of everything, I still cared for him. We still hung out on occasion. One evening in particular, I was invited over while Anthony's mom was out of town for a gathering. I remember things quickly getting out of hand as more guests showed up than Anthony's sister had planned on inviting. A group of guys (about a dozen) showed up, and Anthony wanted them to leave. But these guys wouldn't leave, and none of Anthony's friends volunteered to usher them out, except for me. "I'll go with you," I told him as I grabbed a baseball bat, "if we go down, we go down swinging." And so, together, we escorted those guys out. The baseball bat must have been a great diversion, because we didn't have to use it once that night.

Somehow, no matter the size of the crowd we were with, it felt like it was always just Anthony and me. We shared a deep friendship, and we were always *enough* for one another. Out of all my friends, I connected with Anthony on the deepest level. We always had insightful conversations, and even shared a little spot in the woods where we'd hang out and smoke. One day, he and I were talking about a kid in our class who had everything handed to him and who probably wouldn't have to work a day in his life. I remember Anthony telling me he wished he were a rich kid. I knew I'd never be a rich kid, so I told him I'd rather be a rich dad. Little did I know how profound this offhand comment would become later in my life.

After graduating high school in 2003, we stayed in touch, but after I moved to Oregon in 2006, we lost contact. Towards the end of 2007, when I had moved back to California with Yuka, Anthony called me out of the blue—I hadn't even told him I was back in the state yet. He needed me to pick him up from the hospital and he had no one else to call. I raced over to get him. As he entered my car, he revealed that he had been admitted into the hospital for overdosing. He had been to a party the night before, and he suspected someone had spiked his drink with meth. My heart sank. I knew Anthony; I knew he would have taken the drugs willingly. But his explanation didn't matter to me, because I would always be there for him. On the drive to his mom's house, I stopped at a gas station and bought him a pack of cigarettes. It was in that moment, I realized we had taken completely different paths in life. It broke my heart, and although I didn't approve of his choices, I still loved him like a brother.

After that day, we wouldn't talk again for another four years, but I often wondered about him, and would talk to Yuka about it. She always encouraged me to check on him and advised me that if I didn't, I'd regret it. She always knew what was best for me, though it would be another few years before I followed this advice.

It was around 2011 that I ran into a mutual friend from high school at a local grocery store. We were catching up and he gave me some upsetting news about my best friend. He told me how Anthony had lost his job as an auto mechanic and had become completely addicted to drugs. He was now homeless and stealing from friends who would let him crash on their couch. I was devastated. I confided in Yuka, who once again encouraged me to reach out to him. I finally called him the next day to ask if I could see him. Anthony hesitated; he didn't want me to see him like that. I think he knew his life was slipping away, because he told me he was in bad shape. "I'm really bad, Ace man," he confided. Two days later, I was able see him. I couldn't even recognize him as the chubby kid I had once known—he was gaunt, but worst of all, he looked as though he had given up.

We sat and talked on the sidewalk curb outside the apartment he was staying at, and what followed was Anthony telling me how he'd reached this point in his life. He had been working as an auto mechanic until he'd suffered an injury. The doctor had prescribed him painkillers, which I thought was incredibly reckless, seeing as Anthony was an addict. Always looking for his next high, I knew he had abused the medication. These prescriptions would become his new drug of choice, and he soon lost his job as a result. Coincidentally, this was around the same time his dad had committed suicide. Anthony shakily revealed that the news of his father, paired with losing his job and his injury, had sent him on a rapid downward spiral. He felt hopeless. I offered to help him in any way I could; if he'd just clean up his act, I could get him a job and do whatever it took to get him back on his feet. After I left him that night, he sent me an email.

> *Dude I'm stoked just to get back in touch with you! You grew up much faster than me and I admire you for that. I hope you realize your strengths and see how special you are by now because damn kid you are a hell of a guy... Just wanted to say that because if you haven't realized how valuable you are to humanity yet take a step back and compare yourself to ANYONE we used to chill with.. I hope you see how brilliant you are... Seriously you're a great man and a great friend and father... I saw you shining today like you did in high school and I hope you see it yourself because with your attitude and discipline you can be great at anything... It made me so happy to see you today looking and feeling great. You deserve it.*

I've never deleted his email, and still read it from time to time. Anthony stopped answering my calls and emails afterwards. I knew his silence meant that he couldn't, and wouldn't, get clean. Eventually I stopped trying. I shouldn't have, for this would be the last time I ever saw him.

A few years later, in 2014, I was walking around the mall,

drinking a cup of coffee, when my phone rang. I'm not sure how he had my number, but it was a friend from high school calling me to tell me that Anthony had just died. I softly asked how, but deep down I knew he had overdosed on drugs. My best friend Anthony had relapsed and succumbed to a heroin overdose. I think in my heart, I always knew this day—this call—would come, but I was still so unprepared for it. The news did not feel real to me: I had heard that he was clean for ten months. I had hoped and prayed that he would kick his many addictions once and for all.

The funeral was difficult. I sat alone in the back of the church and cried the length of the service. His little sister shared the story of that wild party, of Anthony and I going out to fight those guys with a baseball bat, and in that moment, I visualized our entire childhood together and felt how close we had been. I remembered that night like it was yesterday. I remembered how I grabbed that bat, ready for battle. I mustered up a smile through my tears, and remembered how we always said we'd have each other's back. But I couldn't have his back anymore; he was gone, and I was crushed with guilt because I felt like I had let him down. From the back of that church, fragments from our innumerable conversations flew through my memory. During one of our more serious conversations in the woods one day, we had begun talking about life, death, the afterlife, and dreams. We made a promise to each other that if one of us ever died, we'd give the other a sign that heaven existed. This thought in particular lingered with me. All I could hope for was that he was in heaven now.

Shortly after the funeral, I began having dreams about Anthony. These dreams became a regular occurrence over the next several months, and I don't think this was a coincidence.

In the dreams, he looked like the familiar, smiling, happy Anthony I had grown up with, and in almost all of them, it felt like Anthony was trying to communicate something to me. However, whenever I woke up, I wouldn't remember the dream enough to understand what he was trying to tell me.

Oddly enough, I had one particular dream about him wherein I could recall every single detail.

In this dream, I stood alone. To my right, I could see a long, dark hallway devoid of light. To my left were the woods that Anthony and I had spent our time in all through high school. The sun was shining over the woods in a way that felt peaceful, blissful. I stood where I was a few more moments, and then suddenly, I saw Anthony. He walked out of that dark hallway, passed right in front of me, and continued into the glistening woods. Just before he vanished in between the trees, he turned around and smiled at me.

Coincidentally, this dream would be the last one I would ever have about him. I knew now, with absolute certainty, that Anthony was okay. That he was finally contented and in a better place. For the first time in a long time, I felt better about Anthony. I felt a sense of peace and closure. I think that, in some way, I blamed myself for not doing more to save him. Maybe I felt like I had given up on my friend too soon, but internally, I knew I had tried. Now, I was comforted with the knowledge that he was free from his pain and I felt a spirit of lightheartedness come upon me.

Throughout your life, you'll find that you make three kinds of friends. There are the friends with whom you share a surface bond. There are friends in which the bond runs deeper, and is unbreakable—this was my relationship with Anthony. Finally, there are friends who stay with you your whole life:

they become your family. That was Abe for me. I love and trust him so much that I made him a part of the family through my son. Abe is a Chinese-American Marine Sergeant and, as I mentioned, the godfather of Noah. His father died when he was around ten years old. We were friends in junior high, but then his mom sent him to Texas to attend a military academy for high school. I would only get to see him during summer vacations, spring breaks, and holidays.

Abe and I built countless memories. He shares my passion for cars: we loved working on them together, building and racing them together, so much so that we would go to the nearby city of Fremont on the weekends and drag race. At eighteen, we purchased our first guns together. It goes without saying that we spent a great deal of time together and he, in turn, spent a great deal of time with my family.

Since my dad had been in the Navy and had also attended a military academy when he was younger, Abe loved coming over to my house to chat with him. They had so many common interests, and Abe would talk to him about joining the military after he graduated; he really looked up to my dad. My dad would listen to Abe while he helped us tinker around on cars in the garage.

Abe still tells me how my dad played an influential role in his decision to ultimately join the military. Since Abe had lost his father at such a young age, he viewed my dad as a father figure. He still loves visiting my parents, and we all consider him to be a part of our family. Abe did join the Marines, as planned, and eventually became a Marine Sergeant. Like any brother would, he visited all the way from San Diego to meet Noah when he was a newborn, right before leaving for Iraq. At the time, we lived in a studio apartment and Noah was just a few days old.

I was the first one of our friends to have a kid, and Abe felt like he should see Noah before leaving. He completed a tour there as the gunner with a tank crew and we stayed in touch. When he returned to California, he asked to go on a second tour to Afghanistan because he wanted to contribute more, but the Marines denied his request so he remained at Camp Pendleton.

The bond that Abe and I share stems from the fact that we both felt like underdogs when we were younger. We figured out how to build our path together, Abe by joining the Marines, and me by becoming a family man. While Abe was stationed in Iraq, he told me about a sign he passed by every day when he left the base for duty. It read, "Complacency kills." He expressed how he respected the fact that I was never complacent in life, and that I was always trying to grow bigger and to better myself.

One of the most memorable moments Abe and I shared together was when Yuka, our kids, and I visited him in San Diego. He took us to the USS Midway Museum, which houses maritime aircrafts. We toured the museum and visited the flight deck, and right there on that flight deck sat my father's decommissioned chopper, the actual helicopter he had piloted when he served our country. Abe and I saw the cockpit where my dad had once sat, and for a moment, we imagined what it must have been like for him. Abe, who is very patriotic like my father, was moved to see this type of history. We stood there, two sons in a sense, admiring a history shared by my father. A real father to me and a father figure to Abe.

He and I have always stayed in touch. Though our topics of conversation these days consist of money, investing, real estate, and the economy, we still find the time to enthuse about cars. We help each other with advice, and are there for each other whenever we need a helping hand. Abe remains a big part of our lives. He fulfills his obligation as a fun uncle to a *tee*, and always comes by the house to bring gifts for Noah and Ariel on birthdays and holidays. Today, Abe is more of a businessman. He owns several companies and dabbles in real estate. We are still best friends but more than that, we are brothers.

CHAPTER 8

Reckless Abandon:
The prodigal son never returns

Standing in the driveway of my parents' house with his shirt off, a cigarette in one hand and a beer in the other, was my older brother Billy. Covered in dirt and grease from fixing his truck, there he stood, in all his redneck glory, as the sun beat down on him and sweat highlighted the smattering of Confederate-styled tattoos covering his body. Here I was, pulling into my parents' house to live with a newborn baby and Japanese wife. This would be Yuka's first impression of my family. She had not met anyone yet, not even my parents. I never asked her what went through her mind that day as we drove up, but I think I was mortified enough for the both of us.

If you've made it this far in my memoir, there's no doubt you've heard me mention my brother. My brother and I are very different—Jekyll and Hyde different. We view the world differently, both socially and ideologically. I absolutely love my brother, but I deplore his behavior and his lifestyle. I'm sure many of his feelings are a result of the times he spent in prison. I always wanted to be close with him, but it's hard to form a bond with someone who has missed almost half of your life. I will never know how it feels to grow up with a big brother because it was stolen from me.

My brother is ten years older than me, and he went to jail for the first time when I was around four years old. He has been behind bars for twenty years of his life. No, he never had a consecutive sentence, but rather a bunch of small sentences that have accumulated over the course of his life. His crimes slowly escalated to the point where he graduated from jail, to prison. He served time at San Quentin and Corcoran, two of the toughest prisons in the country. Charles Manson was housed at Corcoran at the same time as my brother.

I don't like to talk to my brother about his time in prison, so, I've never asked him questions about what he went through or what it was like. I don't know if it's because I'm afraid of what he'll say, or if I just don't care to know the details. He's definitely become more aggressive and fearless and I'd be lying if I said I didn't enjoy having a mean older brother growing up who could be my defender, protector, and enforcer. I felt an odd sense of pride in his tough-as-nails demeanor, because I knew he would do anything for me.

It is often bittersweet, talking about my brother. On one hand, he loves me, he is very loyal, and I'm sure he would take a bullet for me if it came to it. But on the other hand, he has caused me an indescribable amount of pain through his absence. He has been an emotional and financial burden on our family: my parents spent money they couldn't spare for his bail, lawyer fees, and court costs, and life for my brother continued like this for years, because he wouldn't learn from his mistakes.

When I was still in elementary school, I learned that if I answered the phone and it was a collect call, to always accept the charges. It was my brother calling from jail. Growing up, all

I wanted was my big brother, but he was never there. It was hard as a kid for me to process where my brother was and why he wasn't living at home with us. I wanted to play ball with him and do all of the things brothers did together, but I didn't understand what jail was and what he had done not to be allowed to live with us. As I grew older, I slowly understood that my brother was in a place for people who had done bad things.

I recall being in the courtroom the day he was sentenced to four years in prison for drug trafficking, transporting firearms, and driving drunk. I hadn't seen him in a while because he had been in jail awaiting his trial. My parents took me out of school on the lawyer's suggestion that showing family support might help lessen his sentence. So, I sat there, slouched in the back row of the courtroom. I was frightened. Then, my brother entered in a bright orange jumpsuit, escorted by two sheriffs, his hands and ankles shackled together. The judge talked for a while and then rendered his sentence.

My eyes were locked on Billy the entire time. I searched for any sign of emotion on his face as the judge announced his fate, but I saw *nothing*. And just like that, my brother received four years in prison. He didn't look at me or my parents during the sentencing, but I was a nervous wreck. My tear-filled eyes remained focused on my brother as they escorted him out of the courtroom. Just before he reached the door, he turned his head around, looked at me, and gave me a single nod. It would be several months before I saw my brother again.

Towards the end of summer, I was about to enter 9th grade. Starting high school was a big deal for me: I was going to be a freshman and I was feeling abandoned by my siblings: my brother, with his four-year sentence, was gone, and my sister had left to attend college at San Luis Obispo. This would leave me at home alone with my parents and their constant fighting. Since my sister's college was near my brother's prison, Nanny paid for the family to visit them both. I will never forget the way I felt when I saw him in that prison. The guards buzzed me into the little phone room. I sat in the chair and slowly picked up the telephone receiver.

We talked to each other through a thick window of glass. I didn't know what to say; I just stared at him for a minute and held back tears. He looked so different. He was scary, his arms were big and his face, stout. I didn't want to speak because I knew he'd hear in my voice that I was about to cry, but I mustered the strength to say, "You look scary man." He paused for a few seconds, and said "In here, I need to." And that's all he said.

For the next several minutes, I wanted to tell him that I hated him for always being in jail and how much I missed him. I wanted him to know I was going into high school and that I was scared. Now that our sister was off at college, I had nobody at home with me. Mom and Dad had gotten really bad lately and I don't know what to do. I wanted to tell him that I really needed him in my life right now. But of course, I didn't say any of those things. I barely spoke a word. He sensed there was a lot I wanted to say, and he asked me questions about baseball and my girlfriend. I replied in one word answers to bury my emotions.

My brother would write me letters from prison and they meant the world to me. They could never fill the hole he had left in my life from his absence, but knowing he was thinking about me always made me smile before the pain of missing him kicked in. I've never told him this, but I still have a shoebox filled with every letter he wrote me from prison, and I still read them sometimes. They were his only outlet to share his feelings, and reading them, I knew I had a big brother who cared. He remained in prison for four years and served his time, and was released about a week before my high school graduation. I was beaming when I learned that he would come to watch me graduate from high school.

Now, I don't want to make my brother out to be a monster. Yes, he has his issues, but he's done some really great things for me throughout my life. Does it make up for the time we lost as brothers? Of course not, but he has been there for me when he could. He has fulfilled the unspoken rule of an older brother: to defend and protect his baby brother. I remember a time when I was around twelve years old and someone stole my skateboard. I told my brother and he drove around the neighborhood all day looking for whoever had taken it. Skateboarding was sentimental to me because it was one of the things my brother taught me how to do. It meant the world to me my brother cared enough to try and get it back.

So when I had to move back home to my parents' house, my brother knew I was scraping up every cent I could to save for my wife and son. My brother threw me a bone and let me paint houses with him on the weekends. He knew I could use that extra cash. Later on, when I was more established, we flipped a house together. It was another way I hustled to make money for my family. I wanted to repay the favors my brother extended me, and I knew he was good with construction. It was a win-win for everyone and I loved working with my big bro any chance I got.

My brother has had many rowdy incidents where he tried to defend me or protect me. Even as an adult he would step in if he thought someone was trying to take advantage of me.

Although some of his methods were barbaric and he would completely embarrass me at times, I always appreciated the fact he looked out for me. We are still a bit estranged, and though we don't always see eye to eye, there has been and will always be an unspoken love between us.

CHAPTER 9

Talking it Out:
Conversations with my family

Have you ever really sat down and considered the relationships you've had throughout your life? You might think you have your parents all figured out, but then one day your mom or dad opens up to you in a way you never thought possible, and your complete outlook shifts. It's that eye-opening perspective that gives you a newfound appreciation for the people in your life.

Throughout this book, you have listened to me talk about my family. You know the good, the bad, and the ugly, and I want to shed some new light on what I've learned over the years, through various conversations with different family members. Sometimes the way we perceive situations or people as a child is very different from when we view the same scenarios again as an adult. In my younger years, I was resentful for parts of my upbringing, the hardships I had to face, and the shame I had to feel. But when I consider that same life through my adult, fatherly eyes, there are facets that I now perceive differently.

I want to start with my dad, a good man who, for the most part, did the best that he could. My parents recently moved out to the countryside near Monterey, and he loves it there because of its beauty and the convenient, reasonably-priced cost of living. My dad is now 65 but continues to work because my parents were never able to save for retirement. He commutes to work, two hours each way, every day. Our family used to visit my parents often, but now because of distance, we limit our social calls to the holidays.

This past Father's Day was the most recent holiday we visited them. Most of the family had come over—even my brother and his kids. My dad and I were outside looking at his chickens, and he mentioned offhand that he needed to buy some chicken feed. I offered to take him to the supply store; it was Father's Day, and I was looking forward to some one-on-one time with my dad. As we rode through gorgeous green scenery and mature tree-lined roads, he directed my attention to the cluster of family farms we drove past. "When I'm driving through and I see them working the land," he said, "God is here. I can *feel* it." I knew he meant it because he said it with such pride and conviction. I looked at him: he rarely spoke with such emotion. As we rode down the countryside, I took the opportunity to ask him how my mom was doing.

My mom had always had a host of issues but over the past few years, her fears and anxiety had become so crushing that she hadn't been able to leave the house. Early stages of agoraphobia had started setting in, and she couldn't even bring herself to go to the grocery store anymore. My dad told me that the last time he tried to get her out of the house, they hadn't even reached the end of the street before they had to turn around, her panic attack was so bad. It really hurts me to see her this way. They finally have their own home, surrounded by beautiful landscapes, but she can't enjoy any of it and dad has to do things alone.

It should be apparent by now that anxiety and stress-related disorders run rampant in our family. It has become a generational curse, and just about everyone in my family, including myself, suffers from some version of anxiety. I didn't know it as a child, but as it turns out, my dad lived with anxiety too, and Obsessive-Compulsive Disorder. He explained to me that after leaving the Navy, he suffered from unbelievably detrimental anxiety for about fifteen years. As a helicopter pilot in the Navy, he had been in multiple crashes both on land and in the ocean. Consequently, he now has to compulsively check things over and over to be sure they're safe. He had an extensive checklist for when we'd take trips out of town. He needed to check things three or four times to feel safe. Eventually, my dad even admitted that the reason he used to rely on alcohol so much was because it soothed his anxiety.

During this chat, it dawned on me that we had entered new territory. My dad and I were close, sure, but we had *never* opened up to the extent that we were in this moment. There were never deep conversations on anxiety and mental health between us. These were uncharted waters. I thought that, since we were exploring new ground, I could take this opportunity to have a real heart-to-heart talk with him. I would need to initiate the conversation to keep it going because my dad didn't always speak openly about his feelings, but I wanted to ask him a question about my mom. I was apprehensive on how to approach the topic. Cautiously, I mentioned that I recognized that mom put him through so much. I was hoping for more than his typical short answer, so, I simply asked him why he had never left.

He told me he didn't believe in divorce. I paused for a moment, trying to figure out how to continue. Then he told me he wanted to keep the family together. See, he had been with my mom since they were teenagers, and he had been like a father figure to her younger sisters; he'd helped raise them. My mom was the oldest of three girls. In the first chapter, you'll remember how my dad confided in me when I was younger that my mom's father had molested her. What I didn't tell you was that it had been my *dad* who found out.

My mother's little sister had mentioned something to my dad, fifteen at the time, that he found strange, so he immediately confided in Nanny that something suspicious was going on. Had it not been for my dad sounding the alarm, who knows what would have happened. He had rescued my mother and her sisters from their own *father*. He looked at me then, and sincerely expressed how he knew I had had a rough childhood, but in the end he'd decided that keeping the family together took precedence over his own well-being. If it hadn't been for my siblings and me, he would have left; it *would* have been easier to leave, but he held on. I'm not sure what the right decision was, but I told him how grateful I was that he'd stayed.

I told him that even as a kid, I knew my mom was unsteady. He had noticed some of her episodes back in high school when they were around sixteen, and as she got older, the episodes worsened. At the time, he was so in love with her that he just let it go. He confided in me that he'd asked her to get help, to go to therapy, but she refused. He had gone himself, but after a while it became pointless to go without her. As he spoke, I kept myself from interjecting with my own feelings, because my dad never got a chance to open up like this. I just listened. I could feel he really needed to get some things off his chest. Besides, I was learning valuable new things about my family, especially elements of my dad I never knew.

My family was good at keeping their feelings suppressed. That's probably why I do it too. We stopped the talk for a minute to go inside and get the chickens their feed. I wasn't sure if my dad would feel as talkative as he was on the drive up, but surprisingly he was. I told him how growing up, I thought mom had a split personality and when she drank it came out. It's true that I had noticed her voice changing when she drank. He told me that it came out without the drinking, but the drinking did make it worse. Her voice, I remember, became almost childlike. I'd always wondered if she was reverting back to, or finding herself stuck in, a dark place in her childhood when her father had abused her. My dad had never been able to coax her into talking about the details of those events that triggered this undiagnosed PTSD. He tried to get her to open up, but she would just shut down. He learned all he knew from my mom's sister.

He knew she was overwhelmed and overcome by her own past and inadvertently took it out on everyone around her, but even though she had some pretty bad moments, she was still the girl he fell in love with. He told me that he had tried everything with my mom. He tried to be calm, he argued back, and even ignored her but nothing worked. I remember her pushing and pushing his buttons and yelling at him to get out. But my dad stayed. Then he asked me if I remembered the night my mom tried to kill herself by overdosing on my sister's pills. Of course I remembered—how could I ever forget?

That had been the final straw for him, he was done. The hospital called the next day and wanted him to pick her up and he flat out told them no! He told them she was insane, and he didn't want to bring her back home around the kids. He begged them to take her to a facility or somewhere where she could get help or treatment. All the hospital could do was refer her to a psychiatrist. Of course, my dad picked her up, and when he did, he begged her to get help before she destroyed the family for good. My mom, always in a state of denial, retorted that she didn't need help and that everything was his fault. In that moment, and for the first time, he saw her differently. The high school sweetheart he'd fallen for was gone.

As we fed the hens, he went on to tell me that to this day, she has never apologized to him for what she put him and our family through. I could see my dad's demeanor change, and through the cracks in his mask, I saw how hurt and angry he had been for years. He told me, he thought he would take these secrets and feelings to his grave with him, but at least now I would know the truth. I told my dad I was thankful to him for everything he had done for me and for our family. I thanked him for opening up to me in this way. I felt closer to him and honored that he trusted me enough to share these painful memories. This gave me a look into our lives through his eyes. I learned enough to reshape my perspective that day.

Like I mentioned before, my mom and dad are as opposite as opposite can be. While my mom has definitely contributed to the brunt of our family drama, she is also the *heart* of our family. I reflected on the time when Yuka and I had to move into my parents' home after Noah was born. We were brand new parents ourselves and had no *idea* what we were doing. Although I dreaded moving back into my childhood home, I was secretly relieved to be near my mom while I learned how to care for an infant. To our relief, she was *awesome* and provided free childcare for us. This allowed Yuka and I to work and save money without the added financial burden of daycare. She did the same for my brother and sister's children too.

During that time, my mom and I had many conversations on how to change diapers, what to do if the baby got sick, and all the typical things new parents panic about. I never realized it until now, but I think in some way, my mom's presence gave me an extra boost of confidence I needed in the early stages of fatherhood.

My mom and I did share a bond growing up, and it is best expressed in our joint love of the classic children's book *I'll Love You Forever*. She would read that book to me as a child, and my attention was fixated on every word. I couldn't tell you how many times she's read that book to me, and even as adults, we talked about our memories of that book fondly. We would reminisce about the times we shared reading it together, and my mom would always remind me how much she loved me whenever she referenced that book. It didn't dawn on me until recently that I read this book to my own children now. As much as I strove to establish a distance between my painful childhood and my present, I was still passing down some of the fondest memories I hold. It was such a part of the fabric of my life, it feels only natural to read the book to my kids.

Being the type of guy who often buries his emotions, I never thought I'd have the courage to initiate an honest conversation with my mother. I was sitting at home one night, drinking whiskey. It turns out that, whenever I drink whiskey, I somehow lose that part of me that keeps everything suppressed. So, as I sat in my living room and continued to sip this liquid courage, I decided I'd call my mom. Now, I initially called her to talk about something completely different, but at some point, the conversation shifted in a different direction, heading straight for memory lane. Sipping on that whiskey and talking to my mom, I was compelled to tell her how I felt about her behavior over the years.

I very plainly told her the way she had acted while I was growing up was not acceptable. No child should ever have to experience what I had been through. This sudden declaration rattled me: keep in mind, this is the very first time I've ever brought up what I went through as a child to my mom. I have never spoken a word about how I felt, not one.

At first she wouldn't admit to having done anything wrong, using the exact same tactic she had used on my father when he confronted her in the past about her behavior. But I wouldn't let her off the hook. It was time she stopped hiding behind her denial. So, I persisted, and I pushed on, and I reminded her of the night she had tried to kill herself. Every single detail of that night was etched into my brain. What she had been wearing, the smell of burning vanilla incense, and the vivid picture of her being hauled away in the back of a police car. She grew increasingly defensive, refusing to acknowledge her mistakes. Part of me thought there might be a chance that she honestly didn't remember many of those episodes. After all, they happened 25 years ago and she had been drunk during many of them. But I persisted, unleashing every single bitter memory I had.

After vividly recalling countless events, she finally—*finally*—admitted to what she had done. I repeated, over and over again, that no child should see their parent attempt suicide. She responded to me sarcastically by stating she was *so sorry* for being such a horrible mother. But I wasn't trying to make her feel bad, I wanted to show her how much her actions hurt others around her. Finally, she broke down crying and offered me a sincere apology for everything I had endured and witnessed as a kid. She told me all of that was a result of what she had experienced as a child herself. But I didn't hate her or blame her. It was a relief to have *at last* opened her eyes.

This talk with my mom had been long overdue and remains one of the most therapeutic things I've ever done, next to writing this book. After my torrent of emotions had subsided, I felt lighter. I had been holding on to these words for 25 long years, and a weight I didn't realize I'd been carrying suddenly lifted from my shoulders. After we hung up the phone that night, we never spoke of the subject again. The next time I saw my mom a month later, everything was normal. I wasn't sure how to react or feel in light of this apparent normality, but I was still glad to have opened up to the extent that I had that night. With everything said and done, I still loved her.

CHAPTER 10
Overcoming and Self-Reflection:
Release it and let go

When I first began writing this memoir, I think I was looking for an outlet to vent. I still wanted to fan the flames of frustration I feel for my parents to this day. Yet, during the few years it took me to write this book, my mission had changed. Now I know I am writing it to release everything I've pent up within me, and to hopefully help others in the process. Getting all of these memories—the good, the bad, and the ugly—onto paper was *liberating*. I feel free, whereas before, everything had been relentlessly bottled up and used as fuel to propel me out of a lifestyle I knew I didn't want. I refused to repeat a cycle of dysfunction, and that fuel allowed me to give my kids something better than what I'd had. Now that I am finally in a better place, career-and family-wise, I realized I was still carrying this oppressive burden around. It was time to let it go, and this memoir provided me with a therapeutic outlet to do so. I learned so much about myself, my family, and life. I realized I was an overcomer: I had beat every odd, and through all of this self-reflection, I discovered how to release myself from the chains that had bound me for far too long.

I knew my parents, my brother, and my sister loved me. I was fortunate enough to have caring family members like Nanny and aunt Cindi. We could always lean on them for support. I lived in one of the most desired states in our country and I had tons of friends. Sounds great, right? And yet I maintained this internal pain, an overwhelming feeling of dejection that I couldn't quite get a grasp of. No matter how I viewed my situation, I couldn't shake the fact that I felt *cheated*, like my turbulent childhood had set me up for failure as I entered adulthood. I felt like my family's shortcomings and financial problems had taken away untold opportunities from me, and I felt as though I was *owed* something.

I recently had the chance to evaluate many of my past relationships in my life: people I met briefly, mentors, friends, and even family. Some, I just revisited as a fond memory, while others I found myself delving into and reevaluating. In doing this, I recalled lessons I learned that shaped me, struggles I witnessed that strengthened my drive, and misjudgments I never realized I had made. And from this, I grew as a person. Reevaluating my life with new perspectives was very much like... having a garage sale where I cleaned out the junk I'd been holding onto and rediscovered old treasures I never guessed would be so special later on. It was like a spring cleaning for my soul.

I have been tested, treated both poorly and well through various jobs, and I have humbled myself by taking positions others would look down on. Rather than sit on the couch and hope a better job came along, I worked my way up from the life I acknowledged I needed to start from, to the life I have now. I know how it feels to struggle living off minimum wage, and the grit it takes to climb your way up to a salary that can support a family. Becoming a millionaire was merely a happy aftereffect, it was never my initial goal—providing a better life for my family was. But because I refused to settle, I *excelled*. Hard work, persistence, and drive contributed to the success I have had in my life and in my career. This is how I know the way you treat people matters. You should never underestimate a person or undervalue their worth. "Minimum wage" does not mean "dead end," but rather a *starting point*, a first step into greatness, if you'll allow the right mindset.

I have a newfound appreciation for my dad. He taught me more than I ever gave him credit for, and his selfless acts allowed my family to remain together, even throughout the hardest times. My brother made me appreciate the flaws inside all of us. Even though his absence from my life hurt, he still found a way to show me how much he loved me in his own way.

I shared a pivotal moment with my mom and released the anger I had built up inside over the years. I wanted to let her know the way she acted bothered me. I wrestled every day with the idea of forgiving her. I knew forgiveness would be good for me, but that didn't make the task any easier. I was finally able to forgive her after our conversation that night. I love my mom, and though our past issues are still a work in progress, I have to try and focus on the good times. Maybe creating new, better memories will help erase, or at least soothe, old scars.

Everyone has milestones in their life. For some people, it may be graduating college or landing the perfect job, or celebrating that 25-year wedding anniversary. My milestones are a bit more humble and that's okay, because they remain significant to me. Perhaps my greatest achievement was learning to overcome the worst circumstances and turn them into a life I could be proud to live. But most importantly, I think the biggest facet that has changed in me over the years is the way I measure success. I used to find success in materialistic things, like a fancy car or big house in a nice neighborhood. But if my kids are happy and healthy—if my wife is there with me, then that is success in my book.

I don't have a college degree, yet I have found success. I don't live in a mansion, yet I am comfortable. I don't run a billion-dollar empire, yet I can inspire others to never give up. I can share my story, my life, and encourage others to make their own milestones unique to their own truths and experiences. We are our own person. If we don't like our life the way it is, we have the power to change it. Just like I did.

I am an overcomer. I can't remain angry at the trials I have endured, because they reveal to me what my life might have looked like had I never broken the cycle. I refused to give into my victim's mindset. I didn't want my parents' life, and I certainly didn't want my children to live the childhood I had endured. That motivation provided the unbelievably steadfast mindset I needed to change my destiny.

I often think about how close I came to being homeless. I can remember those people on the sidewalk, and the realization they brought me still haunts me. I remember the crushing pain and guilt I felt at Anthony's funeral. I remember the tears I shed in the courtroom when my brother was escorted away to prison. At any point in my life, this could have been me: homeless, dead, or in prison. All I had to do was stop trying. But hard work is often underestimated. Fortitude and willpower are life skills that can't be taught, but must be lived out through an endurance obtained by running your own race. To be honest, I'd say my biggest milestone is surviving and *overcoming*; it allowed me to share my struggles, my journey, and my life with those who need encouragement the most.

ACE BOWERS

This is the true story about a man rising from poverty by sheer determination and grit. Test readers and followers of his weekly blog say "This is Hillbilly Elegy Meets Silicon Valley."

Ace Bowers went from working as a janitor making six dollars per hour to working in Silicon Valley and being worth millions in just five yeras.

This inspirational memoir takes the reader from poverty to wealth and shares just how he did it. A must-read for anyone wanting to know how to make it big in a dog-eat-dog world.

Sometimes it's the mindset that makes things happen.

Made in the USA
Middletown, DE
20 June 2019